B.J. Summers

POCKET
GUIDE
TO
Coca-Cola®

Identifications
Current Values
Circa Dates

FOURTH
EDITION

COLLECTOR BOOKS
A Division of Schroeder Publishing Co., Inc.

On the Cover: Clockwise from top: 1939 serving tray, EX, $375.00 C; Santa Claus string hanger, EX, $55.00 C; Robot with original box, EX, $40.00 C; *Santa Claus is Comin' to Town* pop-up book, EX, $25.00 C; Tractor-trailer truck with Sprite boy, still with original box, EX, $475.00 B; Dale Earnhardt Coke car, NM, $45.00 C; "Please pay when served" counter sign with clock, EX, $850.00 B; Bottle holder for car, EX, $25.00 B; Coke bottle telephone with original box, EX, $25.00 B.

Cover design by Beth Summers
Book design by Lisa Henderson

COLLECTOR BOOKS
P.O. Box 3009
Paducah, Kentucky 42002-3009
www.collectorbooks.com

Copyright © 2004 B.J. Summers

The current values in this book should be used only as a guide. They are not intended to set prices, which vary from one section of the country to another. Auction prices as well as dealer prices vary greatly and are affected by condition as well as demand. Neither the author nor the publisher assumes responsibility for any losses that might be incurred as a result of consulting this guide.

Searching For A Publisher?

We are always looking for people knowledgeable within their fields. If you feel that there is a real need for a book on your collectible subject and have a large comprehensive collection, contact Collector Books.

Contents

Buddy Lee doll in homemade uniform with original patches worn by "Aunt" Earlene Mitchell's father when he worked for Coca-Cola in Paducah, Kentucky, 1950s, EX, $600.00 C. Courtesy of Mitchell collection.

Acknowledgments

I would like to extend my sincere thanks to the following people and businesses without whose help this book would have been impossible.

Gary Metz's Muddy River Trading Co.
Metz Superlatives Auction
P.O. Box 1430
Salem, VA 24153
Ph. 540-725-4311
It's tough to find Coke merchandise better than the items that Gary has at his auctions. Give him a call for the latest auction information.

Antiques, Cards, and Collectibles
203 Broadway
Paducah, KY 42001
Ph. 270-443-9797
e-mail: ACCI2512
Located in historic downtown Paducah, Kentucky, the old Michael Hardware Store is a great place for an afternoon of browsing. Ray Pelley and his friendly staff offer a full line of antiques and collectibles.

Charlie's Antique Mall
303 Main St., P.O. Box 196
Hazel, KY 42049
Ph. 270-492-8175
e-mail: charlies10@aol.com
Located in the historic antique community of Hazel, Ky., on Main Street, this place has it all. The manager, Ray Gough, has some great dealers with a wide variety of antiques and collectibles and some of the friendliest help you'll find. This border town mall can keep even the pickiest collector busy for the better part of a day.

Farmer's Daughter Antiques
6330 Cairo Rd
Paducah, KY 42001
Ph. 270-444-7619
This is a neat shop full of primitives and advertising. Easily located one mile west off I-24 at exit 3.

Chief Paduke Antiques Mall
300 S. 3rd St.
Paducah, KY 42003
Ph. 270-442-6799
This full-to-overflowing mall is located in an old railroad depot in downtown Paducah with plenty of general line advertising, including good Coke pieces, plus a good selection of furniture. Stop by and see Charley or Carolyn if you're in this area.

Collectors Auction Service
Rt. 2 Box 431, Oakwood Dr.
Oil City, PA 16301
Ph. 814-677-6070
CAS offers a great phone and mail auction. Call and get one of their full-color catalogs. You'll be hooked on their services after just one auction.

Riverbend Auction Company
103 South Monroe St.
P.O. Box 800
Alderson, WV 24910

Patrick's Collectibles
612 Roxanne Dr.
Antioch, TN 37013
Ph. 615-833-4621
  If you happen to be around Nashville, Tenn., during the monthly flea market at the state fairgrounds, be certain to look for Mike and Julie Patrick. They have some of the sharpest advertising pieces you'll ever hope to find. And if Coca-Cola is your field, you won't be able to walk away from the great restored drink machines. Make sure to look them up — you certainly won't be sorry.

Pleasant Hill Antique Mall & Tea Room
315 South Pleasant Hill Rd.
East Peoria, IL 61611
Ph. 309-694-4040
  Bob Johnson and the friendly staff at this mall welcome you for a day of shopping. And it will take that long to work your way through all the quality antiques and collectibles here. When you get tired, stop and enjoy a rest at the tea room where you can get some of the best home cooked food found anywhere. All in all, a great place to shop for your favorite antiques.

Creatures of Habit
406 Broadway
Paducah, KY 42001
Ph. 270-442-2923
  This business will take you back in time with its wonderful array of vintage clothing and advertising. If you are ever in western Kentucky, stop and see Natalya and Jack.

The Illinois Antique Center
308 S.W. Commercial
Peoria, IL 61602
Ph. 309-673-3354
  This is a day-long stop. Dan and Kim have restored an old, very large warehouse overlooking the river in downtown Peoria. It's full of great advertising and collectibles. Stop by and see Dan and Kim and their very friendly staff and plan on being amazed.

Rare Bird Antique Mall
212 South Main St.
Goodlettsville, TN 37072
Ph. 615-851-2635
  If you find yourself in the Nashville, Tenn., area stop by this collector's paradise. Jon and Joan Wright have assembled a great cast of dealers who run the gamut of collectible merchandise. Step back to a time when the general store was the place to be, and be prepared to spend some time here.

Riverside Antique Mall
P.O. Box 4425
Sevierville, TN 37864
Ph. 423-429-0100
  Located in a new building overlooking the river, this is a collector's heaven, full of advertising, with lighted showcases and plenty of friendly help. You need to allow at least half a day for a quick look through this place that sits in the shadows of the Smoky Mountains.

Acknowledgments

Bill and Helen Mitchell
4180 State Route 100 E
Henderson, TN 38340
Ph. 901-989-9302
    Bill and Helen have been collecting for years with special emphasis on Coca-Cola, and they are always searching for new finds. So if you have anything that fits the bill, give them a call or drop them a letter.

Richard Opfer Auctioneering, Inc.
1919 Greenspring Drive
Timonium, MD 21093
Ph. 410-252-5035
    Richard Opfer Auctioneering, Inc. provides a great variey of antique and collectibles auctions. Give his friendly staff a call for his next auction catalog.

Wm. Morford
RD #2
Cazenovia, NY 13035
Ph. 315-662-7625
    Wm. Morford has been operating one of the country's better cataloged phone auction businesses for several years. He doesn't list reproductions or repairs that are deceptive in nature. Each catalog usually has a section with items that are for immediate sale. Try out this site and tell him where you got his name and address.

If I have omitted anyone who should be here, please be assured it is an oversight on my part and was not intentional.

Puzzle with 2,000 pieces featuring a potpourri of Coca-Cola items, EX, $55.00 C. Courtesy of Mitchell collection.

All over the globe people know the Coca-Cola logo, and its great taste. What other single product has made such an impact upon our lives? We can have a Coke float, the best of both worlds, ice cream and Coke. And popcorn just doesn't taste right without the taste of a Coke to help wash it down. A picnic without a hot dog and Coke wouldn't be a picnic.

There is a world of us "strange" people out there that have to have their Coke with breakfast, instead of the standard cup of coffee. I've had waiters look at me like I had lobsters falling out of my ears as I ordered my breakfast and a large Diet Coke.

Coke has helped launch many careers in the art and merchandising world. Where would we be without the Rockwell Coke art? And what a coup for the D'arcy advertising agency when the Sprite Boy appeared upon the scene! There is no way J.S. Pemberton could have known the effect his backyard concoction would have on the world in the years to come.

The purpose of a pocket guide is an easy to carry reference. This guide will be convenient for the beginner and advanced collector alike to carry to shows, conventions, and flea markets. The knowledgeable collector is the one with the best "toys" at the end of the day. In this book each price is "keyed" so the source of the price is known. A "B" on the price line indicates an auction price. I usually look at an auction price as a good measure of the value of an item. After all, the true value of a piece is what it will bring on the open market. However some factors have to be considered when dealing with an auction value. Was it a speciality auction? Did two bidders go head to head for the item? Was the item in the auction as a fluke and garnered very little attention? Location and advertising are also things to take into consideration.

"C" stands for the price assigned by a collector. Collectors are usually on top of their collectibles and values. Remember that a collector's favorite piece may be priced on the high side. If a collector has been out of the market for a while the value may reflect past market trends rather than present. "D" stands for the value assigned by a dealer. Remember that a dealer usually is in business to pay the bills. Dealers spend time finding items, researching items, cleaning them, paying taxes, lights, gas, water, and a stack of other bills. So that price will reflect all of these factors.

Location will affect the value assigned an item. Generally speaking items on the east and west coasts will be higher than in the heartland. Always consider the condition of an item when determining value. If a book lists a mint item at one price and that same item appears in fair condition for the same price then it's too high.

Rarity in some cases will help determine value. When will you see another item like the one at which you're looking? If you're looking at the only example you've ever seen and it's in fair condition, but has a healthy price tag, it might be worth the money.

Some other abbrevations for condition of items used in this book are: M-mint, NM-near mint, EX-excellent, VG-very good, G-good, F-fair, P-poor, NOS-new old stock, MRFB-mint removed from box, NMIB-near mint in box, MIB-mint in box, NRFB-never removed from box, NRFP-never removed from package, LE- limited edition.

For the Coke collector there are several good information sources. Coke museums are fantastic locations to see items that haven't been in circulation for years. Try your local bottler, and of course the library. Also check *Schroeder's Antiques Price Guide, B.J. Summers' Guide to Coca-Cola Collectibles*, and *Antique & Contemporary Advertising Memorabilia*.

Our America, Iron and Steel, poster number three in a series of four posters, great graphics but demand for educational material has remained low, 1946, EX, $25.00 C.
Courtesy of Mitchell collection.

*America's Fighting Planes, set of 20 scenes of planes in action, priced at $75.00
each if set is incomplete, 1940s, EX, $1,650.00 C.*

Aluminum die cut, "Drink Coca-Cola In Bottles" in script, truck radiator sign, 1920s, 17½" x 7½", EX.........$375.00 D

America's Fighting Planes, set of 20 scenes of planes in action, priced at $100.00 each if set is incomplete, 1940s, NM...........................$2,000.00 C

Banner, "Be Really Refreshed Around the Clock," 1950s, EX............. $45.00 C

Banner, canvas, featuring a 24 bottle case with area at bottom for the price, 9' tall, EX ....$150.00 C

Banner, paper, "King Size," 1958, 36" x 20", NM..............................$110.00 C

Banner, "Take Coke Home," 108", EX ....$165.00 C

Bottle hanger, rectangular hanger with the message "Thank You for Visiting Us," 1960s, G.......................... $80.00 C

Bottle hanger, Santa Claus holding a bottle with information card about "Twas the Night Before Christmas," fold-out story inside, 1950s, M...............$20.00 C

Bottle hanger, Santa Claus in refrigerator full of bottles, being surprised by small child, 1950s, F................$10.00 D

Bottle hanger, six pack in food basket, 1950s, 8" x 7," EX .... $550.00 C

Bottle hanger, "Ice Cold Coca-Cola King Size," red, white, and green, M, $12.00 C. Courtesy of Mitchell collection.

Bottle topper, Canadian, great graphics by Fred Mizen, "Refresh Yourself," 1926, 13" x 13", EX, $3,600.00 C. Courtesy of Muddy River Trading Co./Gary Metz.

Bottle topper, Bathing Girl, "Drink Coca-Cola Delicious and Refreshing," rare, 1929, VG, $1,800.00 B. Courtesy of Gary Metz.

Bottle topper, woman with yellow scarf and parasol, 1927, 8" x 10", VG, $2,000.00 B Courtesy of Muddy River Trading Co./Gary Metz.

Bottle topper, Bathing Girl, "Drink Coca-Cola Delicious and Refreshing," rare, 1929, G.........................$1,000.00 C

Bottle topper, cardboard, die cut, girl with tray, three dimensional, rare item, 1920s, 11½" x 14", NM ......$2,600.00 B

Bottle topper, plastic, "We let you see the bottle," 1950s, EX ....$475.00 C

Bottle topper, plastic, "We let you see the bottle," 1950s, VG...........$425.00 C

Bumper sticker featuring Max Headroom pleading, "Don't Say the 'P' Word," 1980s, EX ....$10.00 C

Canvas banner, "Take Coke Home," pricing information at bottom, 24 bottle case in center, 9' tall, EX........$425.00 D

Cardboard, baseball scoreboard, made from very heavy stock material, very unusual, 1930s, 30" x 20", EX ....$1,000.00 B

Cardboard, "Big Refreshment Value ... King Size Coke," horizontal poster with lady in straw sun hat, 36" x 20", 1960s, F ....$225.00 C

Cardboard bottle display of girl holding tray, 1926, 11½" x 14", G ....$1,800.00 C

Canvas banner, advertising bottle sales and drinking through a straw, white, red, and black, 70" x 16", 1910, VG, $4,000.00 B. Courtesy of Muddy River Trading Co./Gary Metz.

Cardboard, bather in round blue background, framed and under glass, by Snyder & Black, rare, 1938, 22", NM, $2,700.00 C. Courtesy of Mitchell collection.

Cardboard, bather in diamond blue background pictured with a Coke button and a bottle, framed and under glass, 1940, 23" x 22", NM, $1,700.00 C. Courtesy of Mitchell collection.

Cardboard bottle rack, "Enjoy Coca-Cola," 1970 – 80s, 18", red and white, EX ....$25.00 D

Cardboard, "Buy the case Coke 10 oz. size," black, yellow, and white, EX ....$95.00 C

Cardboard, Canadian trolley card, "Drink Coca Cola, made in Canada," 1920s, 21"x 11", F..................$200.00 C

Cardboard carton insert, "Easy to Serve," 1930s, EX..................$175.00 C

Cardboard, carton insert, "Good with Food" in center, 1930s, EX ....$165.00 C

Cardboard, carton insert, "Good with Food," 1930s, NM ....$175.00 D

Cardboard Christmas display for a holiday bell soda glass, NRFP.........$55.00 C

Cardboard Christmas tree string sign with dynamic wave "Drink...," 1970s, 14" x 24", G ....$32.00 D

Cardboard, clown balancing on a bottle, 1950, G....................................$500.00 C

Cardboard, Coca-Cola polar bear stand up, 6' tall, EX ....$75.00 D

Cardboard, cut out, stand up Eddie Fisher holding a bottle of Coke with easel back, 1954, 5' tall, G, $375.00 B. Courtesy Muddy River Trading Co./Gary Metz.

Cardboard bottle sign with graphics of boys playing around bottle, Canadian, 1930s, 11½" x 11½", NM, $4,700.00 B. Courtesy Muddy River Trading Co./Gary Metz.

Cardboard, cut out, pretty young lady enjoying a bottle of Coke, matted and framed, unusual sign not seen very often, 1936, 15" x 21", F, $475.00 B. Courtesy Muddy River Trading Co./Gary Metz.

Cardboard, "Coke Float" sign, hot air balloons and message blank for "Today's Feature," 22" x 7", EX ....$65.00 C

Cardboard, cut, "Buy Coca-Cola Now For Picnic Fun," shows two couples having a picnic, 1950s, EX............$135.00 C

Cardboard cut-out bottle sign with message board under "Classic" label, NOS, 14" x 45", NM ....$25.00 C

Cardboard, cut out, Coca-Cola policeman, waist up view with "Stop for pause, Go refreshed" ribbon in front, great graphics, hard to find, 1937, 45" x 32", G ....$1,050.00 B

Cardboard, cut out, couple at sundial, "It's Time to Drink Coca-Cola" on edge of dial, 1910s, 29" x 36", G...$3,500.00 B

Cardboard, cut out, "Drink Coca-Cola, The Pause that Refreshes," used as a window display by Niagara Litho Co., N.Y., 1940s, 32½" x 42½", VG.. $975.00 C

Cardboard cut out, model with a bottle and a colorful parasol, easel back, 1930s, 10" x 18½", EX ....$1,650.00 C

Cardboard, die cut, "Drink Coca-Cola, Delicious and Refreshing, Ours is Ice Cold," 1900s, 9" x 19", F ....$495.00 C

Cardboard, die cut, bottle in hand, framed, 1950s, NM, $650.00 B. Courtesy of Muddy River Trading Co./Gary Metz.

Cardboard, cut out, woman shopping with a carton of Coke in her basket, 1944, 17½" tall, near mint, $1,900.00 B. Courtesy Muddy River Trading Co./Gary Metz.

Cardboard, die cut, Coke cherub holding a tray with a glass of Coke, framed under glass, extremely rare, 1908, VG, $4,000.00 B. Courtesy of Muddy River Trading Co./Gary Metz.

Cardboard, die cut, embossed, WWII battleship, framed under glass, 26" x 14", NM..............................$1,300.00 B

Cardboard, die cut, fishing boy and dog with original pond, unusual find, 1935, 36" tall, G.............................$2,650.00 B

Cardboard, die cut, French Canadian featuring bottle in hand, 12" x 16", 1939, NM...............................$600.00 B

Cardboard, die cut, French Canadian string hanger with great graphics featuring woman with a Coke, 1939, 15" x 22", G...................................$1,600.00 B

Cardboard, die cut, girls on a bicycle for two, part of a larger sign, without the background, 1960s, EX..........$275.00 C

Cardboard, die cut of couple with parasol reading sundial, 30" x 36½", 1910s, VG.......................................$5,600.00 C

Cardboard, die cut, poster, "Old Man North" with six pack, "Serve Ice Cold," 16" x 21", 1953, NM..............$275.00 B

Cardboard, die cut, "Serve Coca-Cola" button with candles, EX.........$115.00 C

Cardboard, die cut, service girl in uniform with bottle of Coke, 1944, 25" x 64", EX..................................$600.00 B

Cardboard, die cut easel back of three guys, "So Refreshing," 3' x ½', 1953, G, $175.00 C. Courtesy of Muddy River Trading Co./Gary Metz.

Cardboard, die cut easel back sign of snowman with a glass of Coke, 19" x 32", 1953, EX, $800.00 B.Courtesy of Muddy River Trading Co./Gary Metz.

Cardboard, die cut easel back of boy on bike, 29" x 20", 1950s, F, $260.00 B.

Cardboard, die cut sign, featuring winter girl with Coke glasses, framed and matted, 32" x 19", 1930 – 1940s, EX ....$675.00 B

Cardboard, die cut sign of three ladies at table, 24" x 18", 1951, G.........$450.00 B

Cardboard, die cut, two sided, girl and a glass, 1960s, 13" x 17", EX ....$425.00 B

Cardboard die cut with an ice bucket scene and a glass and bottle in front, 1926, EX ....$575.00 C

Cardboard, die cut with easel back featuring Lionel Hampton, 12" x 15", 1953, EX ....$975.00 B

Cardboard die cut with easel back poster of airman drinking from a bottle of Coke, French Canadian, 12½" x 17", 1941, EX ....$1,550.00 B

Cardboard display, "Pick Up The Fixins, Enjoy Coke," 1957, 20" x 14", NM...$55.00 D

Cardboard, display unit for the "Beverage Dept.," 26" x 36", 1954, EX ....$700.00 B

Cardboard, double-sided hanging mobile, 32" tall, 1957, NM......$425.00 B

Cardboard, die cut, sailor girl with "Take Home" flags, matted and framed, 1952, 11" x 7", NM, $375.00 B. Courtesy of Muddy River Trading Co./ Gary Metz.

Cardboard, die cut easel back sign of a bell glass in ice, 17" x 27", 1930s, EX, $500.00 B. Courtesy of Muddy River Trading Co./Gary Metz.

Cardboard, die cut, "Every Bottle Sterilized," framed and matted, 1930s, 14" x 12", EX, $1,100.00 C. Courtesy of Bill Mitchell.

Cardboard, "Drink Coca-Cola," couple on a beach with a large towel, 1932, 29" x 50", Hayden-Hayden,VG ....$1,800.00 C

Cardboard, "Drink Coca-Cola Delicious and Refreshing," sign with tin frame featuring 1915 bottle on each side, 1910s, 60" x 21", NM ....$1,450.00 C

Cardboard, easel back die cut of woman, "Off to a fresh start," 12" x 27", 1931, EX.........................$875.00 B

Cardboard, easel back French Canadian sign, "Coke Convient," 1948, 18" x 24", NM...$225.00 D

Cardboard, easel back, girls on a bicycle built for two, "Extra Fun Takes More than One," 1960s, F........$55.00 D

Cardboard, easel back or hanging sign featuring a glass of Coke, Canadian, 1949, 12" x 12", EX...............$125.00 D

Cardboard, easel back poster promoting the Kit Carson Kerchief with advertising six pack information, 16" x 24", 1950s, EX.............................$225.00 B

Cardboard, family enjoying Coke, "It's a Family Affair," probably Canadian, 1941, EX .... $400.00 B

15

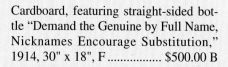

Cardboard, die cut, "The Pause That Refreshes Drink Coca-Cola," super piece and not seen very often, 1937, 34" x 14", VG, $200.00 B. Courtesy of Muddy River TradingCo./Gary Metz.

Cardboard, die cut sign with Coke snowman that folds out from back to produce a three-dimensional effect, probably part of a larger sign, VG, $900.00 B. Courtesy of Collectors Auction Services.

Cardboard, die cut of lady with parasol and a straight-sided bottle of Coke, rare, 1900s, 24" x 27", G, $5,200.00 B. Courtesy of Muddy River Trading Co./Gary Metz.

Cardboard, featuring straight-sided bottle "Demand the Genuine by Full Name, Nicknames Encourage Substitution," 1914, 30" x 18", F .... $500.00 B

Cardboard, horizontal, "Be Really Refreshed," scene of couple in boat on pond, 1960s, 36" x 20", G ....$50.00 B

Cardboard, horizontal, "Drink Royal Palm Beverages Made from Pure Cane Sugar by the Coca-Cola Bottling Company," 1930s, 17" x 11¼", G ....$135.00 C

Cardboard, horizontal, featuring silhouette girl running, "Let's watch for 'em," 1950s, 66" x 32", NM .... $850.00 D

Cardboard, horizontal, "Have a Coke," young cheerleader with megaphone and a bottle, "Coca-Cola" button on right, 1946, 36" x 20", VG ....$250.00 D

Cardboard, horizontal, in original wooden frame, "Coke is Coca-Cola," 1949, 36" x 20", EX ....$675.00 C

Cardboard, horizontal lettered, button right side, "Fountain Service," 1950, 30" x 12", EX ....$450.00 B

Cardboard, horizontal, "Refreshing," woman in white dress at counter with a bottle, 1949, 56" x 27", EX ....$425.00 D

Cardboard, die cut six pack, 1954, EX, $750.00. Courtesy of Gary Metz.

Cardboard, die cut, "Take Enough Home," bottle in hand, 1952, VG, $160.00 B. Courtesy of Muddy River Trading Co./Gary Metz.

Take Enough Home!

Cardboard, die cut, woman 5' tall, holding six pack, EX, $150.00 D. Courtesy of Gary Metz.

Cardboard, horizontal, "Sparkling" bottle in Q of quality in yellow background, original frame, 1957, 36" x 20", EX ....$475.00 D

Cardboard, horizontal, "That taste-good feeling," man drinking from bottle, "Drink Coca-Cola Delicious and Refreshing" button left, 1939, 56" x 27", VG ....$1,000.00 B

Cardboard, horizontal, "Welcome," man in uniform and woman in yellow dress seated on couch with a bottle, 1943, 56" x 27", EX..............................$500.00 C

Cardboard insert, "Serve yourself," with hand holding glass of Coke, 1949, 13" x 11", NM..................................$170.00 B

Cardboard, large horizontal "Mind reader!", woman on chaise being offered a bottle of Coke, EX ....$625.00 C

Cardboard, large horizontal truck side poster featuring mod couple on a motor scooter, 1960s, 67" x 32", VG..$125.00 C

Cardboard, large vertical poster featuring girl with horse, 1938, EX ....$1,000.00 B

17

Cardboard, die cut, woman sitting on bench with bottle, "Delicious and Refreshing, Coca-Cola in bottles," 1900s, 18" x 28½", G, $8,000.00 B. Courtesy of Bill Mitchell.

Cardboard, die cut with attached hangers for wall or window display, Bathing Girl, 1910, F, $1,450.00 B. Courtesy of Muddy River Trading Co./Gary Metz.

Cardboard, dimensional arrow sign, heavy brown cardboard, hard to find, 1944, 20" x 12", G, $150.00 B. Courtesy of Muddy River Trading Co./Gary Metz.

Cardboard, large vertical poster featuring ice skater, 1940s, F ....$80.00 D

Cardboard, light pulls with original strings advertising King Size Coca-Cola, two sided, 1950 – 1960s, M, $35.00; in six pack, "puts you at your sparkling best," round, M ....$55.00 D

Cardboard, lobby poster featuring Clark Gable and Joan Crawford, "Dancing Lady," 1930s, EX ....$1,900.00 B

Cardboard, marching glasses, framed, 34" x 11", 1948, EX ....$725.00 B

Cardboard Merry Christmas price blank sign, 1992, EX............................$6.00 C

Cardboard, oval, string hung, denoting price, German, 1930s, EX......$125.00 C

Cardboard, "Pause," clown and an ice skater, in original wooden frame, 1930s, EX ....$850.00 D

Cardboard, "Play Refreshed," woman on a carousel horse, in original wooden frame, 1940s, EX ....$1,200.00 B

Cardboard poster advertising the Red Hot Summer promotion and a chance to win "A Red Hot Summer Picnic Pack" with graphics of a picnic table complete with various Coke products, 18" x 25", NM ....$35.00 C

Cardboard, easel back die cut window display, 41" x 32", 1939, EX, $775.00 B. *Courtesy of Muddy River Trading Co./Gary Metz.*

Cardboard, "Drink Coca-Cola," couple on a beach with a large towel, 1932, 29" x 50", Hayden-Hayden, F, $625.00 C. *Courtesy of Mitchell collection.*

Cardboard, endorsement featuring Randy Travis with a bottle of Coke, 1990, 12" x 16", NM, $25.00 C. *Courtesy of Sam & Vivian Merryman.*

Cardboard poster, Bathing Girl on rocks at beach, 1938, 30" x 50", G..............................$2,300.00 B

Cardboard poster, "Big Refreshment," girl with bowling ball, 1960s, 66" x 32", EX ....$500.00 C

Cardboard poster, bird on bell and bottle, in aluminum frame, 1954, EX ....$250.00 D

Cardboard poster, "Coke has the taste you never get tired of," with artwork of young girl with 45rpm record and bottle of Coke, 1960s, 36" x 20", EX ....$125.00 C

Cardboard poster, "Coke Time," cover girl with original frame, 1950s, 16" x 27", NM...............................$800.00 B

Cardboard poster, "Drink Coca-Cola," circus scene with performers enjoying a bottle of Coke, difficult to find, 1936, 32" x 50", EX ....$4,500.00 B

Cardboard poster featuring girl at refrigerator, 1940, 16" x 27", EX....$750.00 C

Cardboard poster featuring Hostess Girl, artwork by Hayden, 1935, 29" x 50", NM...............................$2,200.00 C

Cardboard, Enjoy Coke, price blank with the dynamic wave in the center, NM, $8.00 C. *Courtesy of Sam and Vivian Merryman.*

Cardboard, "Enjoy frosty, refreshing sugar free Fresca," with artwork of Fresca bottle and icy glass, 1960s, VG, $200.00 C.*Courtesy of Riverside Antique Mall.*

Cardboard, horizontal, "Coke Party," with three girls around a table enjoying a Coke and sandwich, 1943, EX, $475.00 B. *Courtesy of Muddy River Trading Co./Gary Metz.*

Cardboard poster featuring sports stars Jesse Owens and Alice Coachman with bottles of Coke and the message "Quality you can trust," 1952, EX ....$925.00 B

Cardboard poster, "for good eating," with staggered bottles, 1950s, 36" x 20", G.....................................$250.00 C

Cardboard poster, girl on lifeguard stand, 1929, 17" x 29¾", VG.....................................$1,000.00 B

Cardboard poster, "Good taste for all," 1955, 16" x 27", NM..............$250.00 D

Cardboard poster, "Have a Coke," with skater, 1955, F.......................$500.00 B

Cardboard poster, horizontal, "All set at our house," with boy holding cardboard six pack carrier, 1943, G..$175.00 C

Cardboard poster, horizontal, "Be really refreshed... Enjoy Coke"/"Take Home Plenty of Coke," with scene at swimming pool, 1959, 21½" x 37½", G...$295.00 C

Cardboard poster, horizontal, "Coca-Cola belongs," featuring couple with a picnic basket and a bucket of iced Coca-Cola, 1942, EX......................$750.00 B

Cardboard, horizontal, "Play Refreshed," with cowgirl enjoying a bottle of Coke, still in original gold frame, 1951, EX, $700.00 B. Courtesy of Muddy River Trading Co./Gary Metz.

Cardboard, girl with a bottle, 1940s, EX, $650.00 D. Courtesy of Muddy River Trading Co./Gary Metz.

Cardboard, horizontal poster, "Coke ... For Hospitality" featuring artwork of people at cookout, framed under glass, 1948, 36" x 24", NM, $425.00 B. Courtesy of Muddy River Trading Co./Gary Metz.

Cardboard poster, horizontal, "Coke belongs," young couple with a bottle, 1944, EX ....$700.00 B

Cardboard poster, horizontal, "Coke knows no season," snow scene with a bottle in foreground and a couple of skiers in the background, framed, 1946, 62" x 33", G ....$350.00 C

Cardboard poster, horizontal, "Coke time" featuring three women at table, 1943, EX ....$475.00 B

Cardboard poster, horizontal, "Face your job refreshed," woman wearing visor beside a drill press, 59" x 30", VG........................$800.00 C

Cardboard poster, horizontal, featuring a lunch counter scene, "A great drink with food," Canadian, 1942, 36" x 20", G.............................$550.00 B

Cardboard poster, horizontal, featuring people in a picnic scene with a cooler, 1954, 36" x 24", EX ....$400.00 B

Cardboard poster, horizontal, "Got enough Coke on ice?," three girls on sofa, one with phone receiver, framed, Canadian, 1945, G.................$350.00 C

Cardboard poster, horizontal, "Have a Coke," a bottle in snow, 1945, 36" x 20", G ....$175.00 C

Cardboard, horizontal poster, "You taste its quality," featuring artwork of woman with flowers and a bottle of Coke, framed under glass, 1942, 36" x 20", NM, $1,150.00 B. Courtesy of Muddy River Trading Co./Gary Metz.

Cardboard in wooden frame, "Betty," 1914, 30" x 38", VG, $2,750.00 D. Courtesy of Mitchell collection.

Cardboard light pulls with original strings advertising King Size Coca-Cola, two sided, 1950 – 1960s, EX, $45.00 C.

Cardboard poster, horizontal, "Have a Coke," cheerleader and a bottle, 1946, VG ....$425.00 C

Cardboard poster, horizontal, "Here's Something Good," featuring party scene, 1951, EX ....$350.00 B

Cardboard poster, horizontal, "Hospitality Coca-Cola," girl lighting a candle with a bottle in foreground, 1950, 59" x 30", VG ....$750.00 C

Cardboard poster, horizontal, "Hospitality in your hands," woman serving four bottles from tray, 1948, 36" x 20", F..$115.00 C

Cardboard poster, horizontal, "Lunch Refreshed," 1943, EX ....$1,000.00 B

Cardboard poster, horizontal, "Me too," young boy looking up at large bottle, two sided, 62" x 33", G ....$500.00 C

Cardboard poster, horizontal, "Planning hospitality," with artwork of hand taking bottle from six pack, 27" x 16", EX ....$375.00 C

Cardboard poster, horizontal, "Shop refreshed," 1948, NM..........$1,400.00 B

Cardboard, large horizontal poster, featuring party scene with Coke iced down in a tub, hard to find item, 1952, F, $300.00 B. Courtesy of Muddy River Trading Co./Gary Metz.

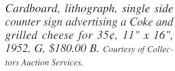

Cardboard, lithograph, single side counter sign advertising a Coke and grilled cheese for 35¢, 11" x 16", 1952, G, $180.00 B. Courtesy of Collectors Auction Services.

Cardboard, "Party Pause," woman in clown suit, 1940s, 36" x 20", G, $350.00 C. Courtesy of Mitchell collection.

Cardboard poster, horizontal, "The pause that refreshes," girl in yellow dress propped against table holding a bottle, in a reproduction frame, 36" x 20", EX..................................$925.00 B

Cardboard poster, horizontal, "The pause that refreshes," girl on a chaise holding a bottle, 1942, 36" x 20", G..$325.00 D

Cardboard poster, horizontal, "The rest-pause that refreshes," three women in uniform, 1943, 36" x 20", EX ....$425.00 B

Cardboard poster, horizontal, "They all want Coca-Cola," girl delivering a tray with four hamburgers, framed under glass, 36" x 20", EX ....$425.00 C

Cardboard poster, horizontal, "Thirst knows no season," woman drinking from a bottle in front of skis, framed, 1940, 56" x 27", EX ....$500.00 C

Cardboard poster, horizontal, "Thirst knows no season," woman drinking from a bottle in front of skis, framed, 1940, 56" x 27", G ....$325.00 D

23

Cardboard poster, "Accepted home refreshment" with graphics of young couple sitting in front of a fireplace enjoying popcorn and bottled Cokes, 1942, VG, $425.00 B. *Courtesy of Muddy River Trading Co./Gary Metz.*

Cardboard, large vertical poster, "Mom knows her groceries," featuring woman at refrigerator, 1946, VG, $450.00 C. *Courtesy of Muddy River Trading Co./Gary Metz.*

Cardboard poster advertising Coke Classic with an inviting message "This pizza calls for a Coke", with fold back to allow for counter top display, 11½" X 14½", NM, $25.00 C. *Courtesy of Sam and Vivian Merryman.*

Cardboard poster, horizontal, "To be refreshed," girl holding a bottle in each hand, in reproduction frame, 1948, EX ....$450.00 C

Cardboard poster, horizontal, "Welcome Home," 1944, 36" x 20", VG............................$375.00 C

Cardboard poster, horizontal, "Why grow thirsty," 1945, 36" x 20", G...............................$125.00 C

Cardboard poster, horizontal, "Zing together with Coke," party scene, cooler on table, 1962, 37" x 21", P ....$110.00 D

Cardboard poster, in original gold frame, "Hospitality in your hands," featuring hostess with tray of Cokes, 1948, EX .... $425.00 B

Cardboard poster, "Join the friendly circle," double sided in original wood gold frame, young people gathered around a Coke cooler on the grass, 1954, G...............................$500.00 B

Cardboard poster, lady about to enjoy a Coke from the bottle, 1957, NM ....$400.00 B

Cardboard poster showing a bottle of Coke in a snow bank, 1946, NM, $550.00 B.
Courtesy of Muddy River Trading Co./Gary Metz.

Cardboard, poster "Coke Time," in original frame, 36" x 20", 1954, EX, $1,200.00 B.
Courtesy of Muddy River Trading Co./Gary Metz.

Cardboard poster, "Come over for Coke," with hostess at serving table with food and bottles of Coke, 1947, 36" x 20", F, $255.00 D.
Courtesy of Collector's Auction Services.

Cardboard poster, large horizontal, "America's Favorite Moment," a couple in a diner booth, each with a bottle, 1940s, 36" x 20", EX ....$295.00 C

Cardboard poster, large horizontal, "Good Pause Drink Coca-Cola in Bottles," 1954, 36" x 20", G ....$500.00 C

Cardboard poster, large horizontal, "The pause that refreshes at home," framed, 1940s, 56" x 27", G...............$275.00 C

Cardboard poster, large vertical, couple and man in navy uniform, 1943, G..$800.00 C

Cardboard poster, part of "Through the Years," Victorian advertising series, 1939, 16" x 27", G ....$750.00 D

Cardboard poster, "Pause and Refresh," great graphics of girl drinking a glass of Coke at soda fountain, counter and dispenser shown, 1948, 41" x 23½", NM ....$2,300.00 B

Cardboard poster, pretty young lady being offered a bottle of Coke and the message "The best of taste," 1956, VG...$350.00 B

Cardboard poster, "Drink Coke in Bottles" in original wood gold frame featuring three boxers, the best known being Floyd Patterson, all three shown drinking bottled Coke, 1954, F, $375.00 B.
Courtesy of Muddy River Trading Co./Gary Metz.

Cardboard poster, horizontal, "Coke for me, too," couple with bottles and a hot dog, 1946, 36" x 20", EX, $375.00 C.

Cardboard poster, horizontal, "Coke Time ... Join the friendly circle," people in pool around cooler on float, 1955, 36" x 20", EX, $375.00 B.
Courtesy of Muddy River Trading Co./Gary Metz.

Cardboard poster promoting a free trip to the NFL Pro Bowl in Hawaii with message and price board at right of graphics, NM ....$12.00 C

Cardboard poster, Reece Tatum of the Harlem Globetrotters holding a basketball with a bottle on top of the ball, 1952, 16" x 27", EX ....$700.00 C

Cardboard poster, seated Chinese girl, 1936, 14½" x 22", NM ....$1,300.00 D

Cardboard poster, "Shop Refreshed," young girl in front of a fountain dispenser enjoying her Coke from a glass, 1948, 41" x 23½", NM.......$2,000.00 B

Cardboard poster, "So Delicious," with ski scene in background and a pretty young lady in the foreground with a bottle of Coke, 1950s, VG ....$475.00 B

Cardboard poster, "Take Coke along," 16" x 27", 1951, EX ....$700.00 B

Cardboard poster, "Talk about refreshing," two young ladies on a blanket at the beach enjoying a bottle of Coke, 1943, VG ....$800.00 B

Cardboard poster, "The best is always the better buy," girl with grocery sack and six pack, framed under glass, 1943, EX .... $975.00 B

Cardboard poster, horizontal, "Hello Refreshment," woman in swim suit coming out of swimming pool, 1940s, 36" x 20", EX, $1,700.00 B.Courtesy of Muddy River Trading Co./Gary Metz.

Cardboard poster, horizontal, "Play refreshed," woman in cap with fishing rig and a bottle, 1950s, 36" x 20", VG, $375.00 C. Courtesy of Mitchell collection.

Cardboard poster, horizontal, "Hospitality Coca-Cola," girl lighting a candle with a bottle in foreground, 1950, 59" x 30", EX, $900.00 D.

Cardboard poster, "The Best of Taste," girl being offered a bottle, 1956, G...$250.00 C

Cardboard poster, "The pause that refreshes," girl on beach in swim suit, add $250.00 if in original aluminum frame, 1950s, 36" x 20", F .....$300.00 C

Cardboard poster, "Things go better with Coke," part of a larger unit, 24" x 20", 1950 – 1960s, VG...........$160.00 B

Cardboard poster, two couples enjoying themselves, Coke in bottles shown, in original gold frame that has been restored, 1954, NM ....$600.00 B

Cardboard poster, vertical, "And Coke Too," 1946, 16" x 27", EX.....$350.00 D

Cardboard poster, vertical, "Coke headquarters," 1947, EX................$395.00 C

Cardboard poster, vertical, "Extra Bright Refreshment," couple at party holding bottles, 33" x 53", EX ....$295.00 C

Cardboard poster, vertical, "Face the sun refreshed," pretty girl in white dress shielding her eyes from the sun with one hand while holding a bottle with the other, 1941, 30" x 53½",VG ..$625.00 C

Cardboard poster, in frame, featuring girl in swim suit with a bottle of Coke, "Yes," 1947, 15" x 25", F, $375.00 B. Courtesy of Muddy River Trading Co./Gary Metz.

Cardboard poster, "Lunch Refreshed" with great graphics of waitress serving bottled Coca-Cola and sandwiches from a tray, difficult to locate, 1948, 16" x 27", NM, $1,600.00 B. Courtesy of Muddy River Trading Co./Gary Metz.

Cardboard poster, horizontal, "The drink they all expect," couple getting ready to entertain with finger sandwiches and iced bottles, 1942, NM, $600.00 B. Courtesy of Muddy River Trading Co./Gary Metz.

Cardboard, poster, vertical, featuring girl on sidewalk, "So easy to carry home," 1942, 16" x 27", EX .... $800.00 D

Cardboard, poster, vertical, featuring girl with a tennis racquet, 1945, EX .... $525.00 D

Cardboard poster, vertical, "Have a Coke, Coca-Cola," couple at masquerade ball, framed under glass, rare item, VG .... $550.00 C

Cardboard poster, vertical, "Have a Coke," girl with bottle in each hand in front of drink machine, 1940s, 16" x 27", EX .... $350.00 C

Cardboard poster, vertical, "Home Refreshment," framed under glass, EX .... $1,800.00 C

Cardboard poster, vertical, "Join me," fencer resting against a chest cooler with a bottle, in reproduction frame, 1947, 16" x 27", EX .... $775.00 B

Cardboard poster, vertical, "Just Like Old Times," 1945, 16" x 27", EX .... $400.00 C

Cardboard poster, vertical, "Let's have a Coke," cooler and majorette, 1946, 16" x 27", EX .... $350.00 C

Cardboard poster, "Play refreshed," young lady in tennis attire sitting on a Coke lift top floor cooler, enjoying a bottle of Coke, 1949, NM, $2,700.00 B. Courtesy of Muddy River Trading Co./Gary Metz.

Cardboard poster, MGM actress Florine McKinney sitting on patio table, 1935, 13½" x 30", F, $425.00 B. Courtesy of Muddy River Trading Co./Gary Metz.

Cardboard poster, vertical, "On the refreshing side," couple with bottles, 1941, 30" x 50", VG .... $600.00 B

Cardboard poster, vertical, "Right off the ice," girl at ice skating rink, 1946, 16" x 27", EX .... $400.00 C

Cardboard poster, vertical, "So Easy," woman illuminated by candle getting ready for small gathering, 1950s, VG .... $450.00 C

Cardboard poster, vertical, "So Refreshing … Drink Coca-Cola," 1941, EX .... $750.00 B

Cardboard poster, vertical, "Start Refreshed," couple at roller skating rink, 1943, 16" x 27", EX ...... $375.00 C

Cardboard poster, vertical, "Take some home today," in original wooden frame, 1950s, 16" x 27", VG .... $650.00 C

Cardboard poster, vertical, "The drink-they all expect," showing full length artwork of couple preparing for entertaining, 1942, EX .... $700.00 B

Cardboard poster, vertical, "The drink they all expect," similar to horizontal poster of this year but showing full length artwork of couple preparing for entertaining, 1942, F .... $150.00 C

Cardboard poster, pretty red headed young lady at pool's edge with a bottle of Coke, message reads "Cooling Lift," 1958, EX, $500.00 B. Courtesy of Muddy River Trading Co./Gary Metz.

Cardboard poster with graphics of snowman with his arm around an over-sized bottle of Coke, Canadian and difficult to find, 1941, 16" x 27", NM, $225.00 B. Courtesy of Muddy River Trading Co./Gary Metz.

Cardboard poster, "Now for a Coke," 36" x 20", 1951, NM, $1250.00 B. Courtesy of Muddy River Trading Co./Gary Metz.

Cardboard poster, vertical, "Things go better with Coke," scene of food and Coke, 1960s, F ....$125.00 C

Cardboard poster, vertical, "Thirst knows no season," couple building a snowman, graphics are great, 1942, 30" x 50", NM.............................$725.00 C

Cardboard poster, vertical, with girl on ping pong table, framed under glass, Canadian, 14" x 28", VG ....$600.00 D

Cardboard poster, vertical, with large bottle in foreground and places and events in background, "58 Million a Day," 1957, 17½" x 28½", F.$125.00 D

Cardboard poster, vertical, with large bottle in foreground and places and events in background, "58 Million a Day," 1957, 17½" x 28½", P....$75.00 D

Cardboard poster, "Wherever thirst goes," great graphics of girl in rowboat with a bucket of iced Coca-Cola, 1942, EX ....$550.00 B

Cardboard poster, "Wherever you go," travel scenes in background, 1950s, EX ....$250.00 C

Cardboard poster with entertainer singing in front of microphone with bottle, "Entertain your thirst," 1940s, 36" x 20", EX...................................$600.00 B

Cardboard poster string hanger, "Familiar refreshment," bottle of Coke and plate with sandwich, 1940, 14" x 31", F, $250.00 B. Courtesy of Muddy River Trading Co./Gary Metz.

Cardboard poster, three women, "Friendly pause," 1948, 16" x 27", NM, $1,500.00 B. Courtesy of Muddy River Trading Co./Gary Metz.

Cardboard poster, "Time out for food and drink," showing pretty young lady enjoying a bottle of Coke, 1938, G, $625.00 B. Courtesy of Muddy River Trading Co./Gary Metz.

Cardboard poster with Johnny Weissmuller and Maureen O'Sullivan sitting on springboard, "Drink Coca-Cola, Come up smiling," 1934, 13½" x 29½", EX .... $2,900.00 C

Cardboard poster with the message "Home refreshment" featuring a young lady and a military man, in the original wood frame by Kay Displays, 1944, EX ....$1,300.00 B

Cardboard poster, woman sitting wearing a broad brimmed hat with flowers, holding a Coca-Cola 5¢ bamboo fan and glass, framed, 1912, EX ....$4,750.00 D

Cardboard poster, woman with different size cartons, and the message "Get Both sizes in Cartons," 1956, NM $500.00B

Cardboard poster, "Zing for your supper with ice cold Coke," young cartoon man in early version space suit with food and a bottle, 1960s, EX.................$135.00 C

Cardboard, rack sign featuring Eddie Fisher on radio, 1954, 12" x 20", EX ....$135.00 C

Cardboard, rack sign for 12 oz. cans with large diamond cans, 1960s, NM...$75.00 D

Cardboard poster, vertical, "Coke Time," head shot of woman, bottle in hand, and various sports activities, 1950s, F, $225.00 C. Courtesy of Mitchell collection.

Cardboard poster, vertical, "Coke Time," in original wooden frame, EX, $950.00 B. Courtesy of Muddy River Trading Co./Gary Metz.

Cardboard poster, two young ladies with a globe and a bottle of Coke, and the message "Here's to our G.I. Joes," 1944, G, $600.00 B. Courtesy of Muddy River Trading Co./Gary Metz.

Cardboard, Red Hot Summer game cup display poster, 1994, 20" x 12", NM ....$35.00 C

Cardboard showing woman picking up a carton of Coke from store rack, with the message "Easy To Take Home," 1941, EX ....$800.00 B

Cardboard sign with graphics of bottle opening and coke emerging, message "drive with real refreshment," 1999, 8" x 8", NM..............................$10.00 C

Cardboard, stand up, "For the emergency shelf," folds in middle, EX ....$285.00 B

Cardboard, St. Louis Fair, woman sitting at table with a flare glass that has a syrup line, 1909, G..............$4,700.00 C

Cardboard, "Stop ... Go refreshed" poster, framed under glass, 16" x 27", 1950s, VG ....$185.00 C

Cardboard, string hung die cut "Float with Coke," 1960s, 10" dia., EX .... $85.00 C

Cardboard, 3-D, "Boy oh Boy," pictures boy in front of cooler with a bottle in hand, 1937, 36" x 34", VG......$850.00 C

Cardboard poster, vertical, "Drink Coca-Cola" upper left hand corner, girl on towel at beach, bottle, framed under glass, rare, hard to find, 1930s, 30" x 50", EX, $1,700.00 B. Courtesy of Muddy River Trading Co./Gary Metz.

Cardboard poster, vertical, "Drink Coca-Cola" on button, girl at stadium in the fall holding a program and a bottle, framed under glass, 1940, 30" x 50", EX, $1,400.00 B. Courtesy of Muddy River Trading Co./Gary Metz.

Cardboard poster, vertical, "Home refreshment," woman holding a bottle with the refrigerator door ajar, 1950s, 16" x 27", NM, $550.00 B. Courtesy of Muddy River Trading Co./Gary Metz.

Cardboard, trolley car sign, "Anytime Everywhere … The Favorite Beverage," 21" x 11", 1910s, EX ....$1,900.00 C

Cardboard, trolley car sign, "Coca-Cola 5¢ at fountains," 20½" x 10¾", 1905, G..$1,850.00 B

Cardboard, trolley car sign, "Drink Coca-Cola Delicious and Refreshing," matted and framed, 21" x 11", 1910s, EX ....$675.00 B

Cardboard, trolley car sign, matted and framed, "Around the corner from any-where," 1927, EX................$2,600.00 B

Cardboard, trolley car sign, "Relieves fatigue, Sold everywhere," good graph-ics, 1907, 20" x 10¼", F .....$3,400.00 B

Cardboard, truck poster, "Refreshing new feeling," 1960s, 67" x 32", EX ....$135.00 C

Cardboard, truck poster, "Refreshing new feeling," woman in pool with straw hat, 67" x 32", 1960s, NM ......$135.00 C

Cardboard, truck poster, "Yield to the children," 67" x 32", 1960s, NM ....$95.00 C

Glass and metal light-up, "work safely work refreshed," cardboard insert, with original packing box, 1950s, 16" x 16", EX, $675.00 B. Courtesy of Muddy River Trading Co./Gary Metz.

Glass and metal, reverse painted message "Drink Coca-Cola," original chrome frame and chain, white on red, 20" x 12", 1932, EX, $3,500.00 B. Courtesy of Muddy River Trading Co./Gary Metz.

Glass and wire, sign, 14" dia., 1965, EX, $400.00 B. Courtesy of Muddy River Trading Co./Gary Metz.

Cardboard, vertical, "Coke Time," bottle in hand with woman's face, "Drink…" button in lower center, 1954, 16" x 27", EX ....$325.00 D

Cardboard, vertical, "Come and get it," western dinner gong behind a bottle, "Drink…" button in lower right, 1952, 16" x 27", EX ....$300.00 C

Cardboard, vertical double sided sign, "The best of taste" on one side, "Enjoy the quality taste" on the other, 1956, 56" x 27", VG ....$250.00 D

Cardboard, vertical sign featuring a burger plate and a bottle of Coke, "A great combination," EX..........$110.00 C

Cardboard, vertical, "So Refreshing," Autumn Girl in art work, 1940, 16" x 27", EX...................................$575.00 C

Cardboard, "Welcome friend," red and white lettering on simulated oak background, 1957, 14" x 12", VG..$250.00 C

Cardboard with girl at a refrigerator holding a bottle of Coke and proclaiming "Home Refreshment" on one side and kids at a picnic cooler with bottled Cokes on the reverse side, 1950, NM ....$675.00 B

Kay Displays, "Work Refreshed" with "Education" center medallion, 23" x 11½", 1940s, EX, $375.00 B. *Courtesy of Muddy River Trading Co./Gary Metz.*

Kay Displays, metal and wood soda glass sign, 9" x 11½", 1930s, NM, $825.00 B. Courtesy of Muddy River Trading Co./Gary Metz.

Light-up double-sided halo type sign with cup insert, "Same quality as bottled Coca-Cola now in cups," 1950s, 16" dia., EX, $2,400.00 B. Courtesy of Muddy River Trading Co./Gary Metz.

Cardboard with graphics of bottle opening and Coke emerging, message "drive with real refreshment," 1999, 8" x 8", NM ....$10.00 C

Cardboard with original string hanger and graphics of bottle, probably Canadian, 13" x 33," EX ....$475.00 B

Cardboard with young woman in the moonlight with the message "The pause that refreshes," 1939, G..........$550.00 B

Celluloid bottle, "Drink Coca-Cola Delicious and Refreshing," 1900s, 6" x 13¼", VG........................... $2,300.00 C

Celluloid disc, foreign, Spanish, rare, yellow and white on red, 1940s, 9", NM.......................................$350.00 D

Celluoid disc sign, string hanger, similar to white version below but in hard-to-find red, 1942, 9" dia., G..$3,700.00 B

Celluloid over tin, "Refresh Yourself Drink Coca-Cola," probably manufactured in the U.S.A. for use in Canada, yellow & white on red with green frame, 1930s, 11¾" x 6", EX .... $1,800.00 C

Light-up double-sided sign, with fishtail logo, 3 x 20" x 9", 1960s, EX, $350.00 B. Courtesy of Mu River Trading Co./Gary Metz.

Light-up, "Work Safely" sign, 15½" square, 1950s, EX, $775.00 B.Courtesy of Muddy River Trading Co./Gary Metz.

Light-up halo type sign, double sided with "Have a Coke Here" on one side and "In Bottles" on the other side, plastic and metal, 1950s, 16" dia., near-mint, $1,400.00 B. Courtesy of Muddy River Trading Co./Gary Metz.

Celluloid, round, "Coca-Cola," white lettering on top of a bottle in center with red background, 1950s, 9" dia., EX .... $250.00 C

Celluloid, round, hanging on easel back, "Delicious Coca-Cola Refreshing," white and black lettering on red background, 1940, VG ....$180.00 D

Celluloid round sign with graphics of bell glass, scarce item, "Pause Go Refreshed," 1942, 9" dia., EX ....$4,700.00 B

Composition round sign, "Pause ... go refreshed," heavily embossed with wings showing bottle in hand at the center, 1941, 9½" dia., NM ......$2,100.00 B

Countertop light-up sign, "Drink Coca-Cola" with glass in spotlight at bottom center, back lit with red and white bulbs, manufactured by Brunhoff Mfg. Co., red and white, 1930s, 12" x 14", EX ....$6,200.00 B

Metal and glass light-up counter sign, waterfall motion, "Pause and Refresh," 1950s, EX, $1,150.00 B. Courtesy of Muddy River Trading Co./Gary Metz.

Masonite, die cut, pretty blond girl holding a glass and a bouquet of flowers, 1940s, 42" x 40", VG, $550.00 B. Courtesy of Muddy River Trading Co./Gary Metz.

Masonite, die-cut sign with teenagers on records, hard to find, 1950s, 12", EX, $2,200.00 B. Courtesy of Muddy River Trading Co./Gary Metz.

Dale Earnhardt die-cut life-size stand up with fold out stand in back. The price on these was in the $10.00 – 15.00 range the day before his death; the day after it was in the $100.00 – 125.00 range. The price will probably come back down within the next few years, EX .... $100.00 C

Decal, bottle in hand, EX ....$35.00 D

Decal, "Drink Coca-Cola in Bottles," framed, 1950s, 15" x 9", EX ....$50.00 D

Decal, "Drink Coca-Cola in Bottles," on glass, framed, 1950s, 15" x 18", EX ....$95.00 C

Decal, "Drink" emblem on triangle, "Ice and Cold" by bottle, 1934, 15" x 18", NM ....$165.00 D

Decal, fishtail logo with sprig of leaves, EX ....$45.00 C

Decal for Fanta root beer, "Enjoy Fanta Root Beer," 8" x 4", 1960s, EX......$5.00 C

Decal, "Thank You Come Again," on bow tie emblem, foil, 1950s, NM...$35.00 D

Die cut Coca-Cola bottle sign, 1951, 6' tall, G .... $550.00 D

Metal, double-sided rack sign, "Serve Coca-Cola Sign of Good Taste," 17" x 10", 1960s, G, $110.00 C. *Courtesy of Muddy River Trading Co./Gary Metz.*

Metal curb sign insert advertising the eight bottle carton with the message "Take Home 8 Bottle Carton" and graphics of eight bottle pack, eight bottle advertisements are difficult to find, 1960s, 20" x 28", EX, $4,000.00 B. *Courtesy of Muddy River Trading Co./Gary Metz.*

Metal, double-sided, "In any weather Drink Coca-Cola," thermometer on one side fits on outside of screen door, while the "Thanks Call Again" fits on the inside of the door, rare, 1930s, EX, $2,100.00 B. *Courtesy of Muddy River Trading Co./Gary Metz.*

Die cut original artwork of boy with Coke glass, framed under glass, 1940s, 8" x 14", EX ....$1,375.00 C

"Drink Coca-Cola, Cures Headache...Relieves Exhaustion at Soda Fountains 5¢," framed under glass, 1890 – 1900s, VG ....$1,500.00 B

Fountain service sign, two sided, features early dispenser, red on yellow background, 1941, 25" x 26", NM ....$2,200.00 B

Glass and metal, light up counter sign, "Please Pay When Served," red and white, 20" x 12", 1948, VG.......................................$2,000.00 B

Glass and plastic, motion light, 11½" dia., 1950s, NM.....................$675.00 B

Glass front light-up, "Please Pay When Served," located on top of courtesy panel, 1950s, 18" x 8", VG ....$600.00 D

Glass front light-up sign that has an illusion of movement, featuring "Have a Coke," arrow and a cup of Coke, hard-to-find item, 1950s, 17" x 10" x 3", NM ....$1,400.00 B

Glass light-up, "Have A Coke, Refresh Yourself" with red arrow, 1950s, 10" x 17", NM.............................$1,300.00 C

Metal, double-sided sidewalk sign, Canadian, 1949, 58" x 28", NM, $1,200.00 D.

Metal, "Drink Coca-Cola, Delicious and Refreshing," bottle on left side, "The Icy-O Company Inc., Charlotte, N.C.," EX, $850.00 B. Courtesy of Muddy River Trading Co./Gary Metz.

Metal footed revolving four panel light up sign in likeness of lantern, 1960s, 20" tall, NM, $1,600.00 B. Courtesy of Muddy River Trading Co./Gary Metz.

Glass, oval, "Drink Coca-Cola 5¢," silver lettering on maroon colored background, 1906, 9" x 6¾", VG......................................$2,400.00 C

Glass, round, "Drink Coca-Cola 5¢," gold trademark with blue background, 1900s, 8" dia., F................. $2,200.00 D

Heavy paper die cut of woman in heavy cold weather coat with hood, advertising Coke in a glass, framed and matted, "Round the world, 1944," Litho in USA, 1944, EX......................$295.00 D

Illusion light-up sign, plastic front, 1960s, 11", NM..................... $775.00 B

Kay Displays, wood and wire sign with golfing theme, 1930 – 1940s, EX...$400.00 C

Kay Displays, wood and wire sign with scene of girl fishing, 1930 – 1940s, EX...$400.00 C

Kay Displays, wood sign with airplane, 27" x 7", 1940s, EX ....$650.00 B

Light-up, "Beverage Department" with fishtail logo, 1960s, 50" x 14", VG..$250.00 D

Light-up counter sign featuring 20 oz. bottle, NOS in original box, 1990s, 12" x 13", EX................................$225.00 C

39

Original artwork of gouache on board, showing actors on western set enjoying a Coke break, 22" x 14", 1950 – 1960s, NM, $1,000.00 B. Courtesy of Muddy River Trading Co./Gary Metz.

Paper, calendar top, girl sitting on slat back bench wearing a large white hat with a red ribbon and drinking from a bottle with a straw, framed, 1913, 16" x 24", G, $4,500.00 C.

Paper, bottler's calendar advance print, Garden Girl on a golf course, framed under glass, rare, 1919, NM, $8,200.00 C. Courtesy of Mitchell collection.

Light-up counter sign with dispenser, 1959, 12"w x 27"t x 15"d, G ......$950.00 B

Light-up countertop sign, featuring bottle with message "Always feels right Always Coca-Cola," NOS, 12" x 13", 1990s, NM.............................$250.00 C

Light-up glass and plastic counter-top sign, with logo at each end, 18½" x 8", 1950s, NM.......................... $2,600.00 B

Light-up metal and plastic sign with flourescent double-sided message board that carries the message on one side "Baby Needs / Drink Coca-Cola / Toys – Gifts" and on the reverse side "cosmetics & prescriptions" with arrow pointing the way, 1950s, 28" x 23", EX ....$1,900.00 B

Light-up metal and plastic sign with flourescent double-sided message board that carries the message on one side "Thank You / Drink Coca-Cola / Call Again" and on the reverse side "fountain and prescriptions," 1950s, 28" x 23", NM.............................. $1,800.00 B

*aper poster featuring a bottle of Coke on snow, printed
n heavy outdoor paper, 1942, 57" x 18", EX, $130.00 B.
ourtesy of Muddy River Trading Co./Gary Metz.*

*Paper, two women drinking from bottles sitting in
front of an ocean scene with clouds in the sky,
1912, 16" x 22", VG, $4,750.00 C.*

*Paper poster featuring
bottle and icicles with
the message "refresh-
ing," 1957, 57" x 19",
NM, $400.00 B. Courtesy
of Muddy River Trading
Co./Gary Metz.*

Light-up, plastic and glass, "Pause and
Refresh," "Quality carries on" on right
side with bottle in hand, same artwork
as appears on fans of this vintage,
1940s, 19" x 15½", EX ....$675.00 B

Light-up, plastic and metal, round, dou-
ble sided, "Drink Coca-Cola Sign of
Good Taste," 1950, 16" dia.,
EX ....$475.00 C

Light-up, plastic, rotating, "Shop
Refreshed Drink Coca-Cola," 1950s,
21" tall, G..............................$525.00 B

Light-up sign featuring a young lady
enjoying a bottle of Coke in a witch's
costume with a jack-o-lantern on the
table, unusual item, 1940s, 10" x 8",
NM .... $2,000.00 B

Light-up sign, "Have a Coke" with
beveled edge, 18" x 12", 1940 – 1950s,
EX ....$775.00 B

Light-up starburst behind Coke cup, 14"
x 16", 1960s, EX .... $500.00 C

Light-up "Work Safely" plastic with
cardboard insert and Coca-Cola paper
cup on left of lower panel, 1950s, 15½"
square, G ....$725.00 B

Paper, printer's proof of 1923 cardboard poster, found in the estate of Mrs. Diana Allen who posed for this in 1922, 15¾" x 25", 1922, EX, $8,000.00 B. Courtesy of Collectors Auction Services.

Paper, "That taste-good feeling," boy with Coca-Cola and hot dog, 1920s, EX, $650.00 B. Courtesy of Muddy River Trading Co./Gary Metz.

Paper, window display, di cut, glass shaped, "Drin Coca-Cola," rare, 12" 20", EX, $1,800.00 B. Cou tesy of Muddy River Tradin Co./Gary Metz.

Masonite and aluminum cooler sign with arrow through outside circle, 1940s, M................................$550.00 C

Masonite, "Delicious & Refreshing," girl with bottle, 1940s, F..........$70.00 D

Masonite, diamond sign with bottle in spotlight at bottom, yellow and white on red, 42" x 42", 1946, NM...... $950.00 B

Masonite, horizontal, "Drink Coca-Cola Fountain Service," fountain heads on outside of lettering, 1930 – 40s, 27" x 14", EX................................$1,200.00 B

Masonite sign, with waitress serving four glasses of Coke, 37" x 39", 1940s, EX ....$250.00 C

Metal and glass, light-up cash register topper, 1940 – 1950s, EX.......$950.00 B

Metal, building sign, "Drink Coca-Cola," 1950 – 1960s, 48" dia., EX ....$250.00 D

Metal, Canadian carton rack, features sign at top advertising "Take home a carton 30¢," 1930s, 5' tall, EX ....$450.00 D

Metal, "Coca-Cola Sold Here," store sign, red and white, 1920s, G.............$850.00 B

Paper, "Sun-worship" center magazine ad, 1960s, EX, $75.00 C. Courtesy of Mitchell collection.

Plywood, double sided, "Slow School Zone Enjoy Coca-Cola, Drive Safely," 1950 – 1960s, EX, $950.00 C.

Plywood and metal arrow and bottle sign "Drink Coca-Cola Ice Cold," 1939, 17" dia., G, $425.00 C.

Metal, cooler panel insert, "Serve Yourself, Please Pay the Clerk," yellow & white on red, 1931, 31" x 11", G ....$140.00 B

Metal curb sign, double-sided metal sign in sidewalk sign, with fishtail sign over bottle, 22½" x 33" x 24", VG ....$425.00 C

Metal curb sign insert advertising the King Size carton, message reads "Take home a carton...Big King Size," 1961, 20" x 28", NM....................$1,500.00 B

Metal curb sign insert with fishtail logo at top and the message "Take home a carton" and graphics of a regular size six pack at bottom, 1959, 20" x 28", EX ....$1,300.00 B

Metal double-sided flange sign featuring graphics of a Coke bottle and the message "Enjoy Coca-Cola in Bottles," difficult sign to locate, 1954, EX ....$4,500.00 B

Metal double-sided flange sign with the message "Hart Cafe," 1950s, EX .... $1,800.00 B

Porcelain button sign, "Drink Coca-Cola," 2' dia., NM, $375.00 B. Courtesy of Muddy River Trading Co./Gary Metz.

Plywood, soda person with a glass of Coke, center part of festoon, 1930 – 1940s, EX, $375.00 B. Courtesy of Muddy River Trading Co./Gary Metz.

Porcelain, fountain service sign, 28" x 12", EX, $800.00 B. Courtesy of Muddy River Trading Co./Gary Metz.

Metal double-sided flange sign with the message "Ice Cold" at the bottom next to a glass of Coke, 1954, EX ....$2,500.00 B

Metal double-sided flange sign with the message "Soda," 1950s, EX ....$3,300.00 B

Metal, double-sided fountain service sign, 1934, 23" x 26", NM .... $1,600.00 D

Metal, double-sided, "In any weather Drink Coca-Cola," thermometer on one side fits on outside of screen door, while the "Thanks Call Again" fits on the inside of the door, rare, 1930s, G...$1,800.00 B

Metal double-sided triangle sign hung from overhead wrought iron holder with great filigree at top, 1937, EX .... $4,000.00 B

Metal, "Drink Coca-Cola, Delicious and Refreshing," bottle on left side, "The Icy-O Company Inc., Charlotte, N.C.," F ....$475.00 D

Porcelain, double-sided fountain sign, featuring an early dispenser, 25" x 26", 1941, EX, $2,200.00 B. Courtesy of Muddy River Trading Co./Gary Metz.

Porcelain, double-sided dispenser sign with metal frame, 28" x 27", G, $850.00 B. Courtesy of Collectors Auction Services.

Porcelain, shield sign, "Drink Coca-Cola," white and yellow and red, 36" x 24", 1942, EX, $325.00 B. Courtesy of Muddy River Trading Co./Gary Metz.

Metal, "Drink Coca-Cola in Bottles," original bent wire frame and stand, white lettering on red background wire is painted white, 1950s, EX.................$300.00 C

Metal, "Drink Coca-Cola in Bottles," original bent wire frame and stand, white lettering on red background wire is painted white, 1950s, G......$175.00 C

Metal, "Drink Coca-Cola," with bottle at right of message, 1950s, 54" x 18", EX ....$300.00 C

Metal, fishtail, painted, "Coca-Cola Sign of Good Taste," bottle on right side of sign, 31¾" x 11¾", G........$235.00 C

Metal, fishtail, painted, horizontal, "Coca-Cola, Sign of Good Taste," white lettering on red background on white frame with green stripes, 1960s, 46" x 16", EX...................................$245.00 C

Metal, flange, Italian, American-made sign, white & yellow on red, 1920s, 16" x 12", NM............................$1,500.00 B

Metal, French Canadian carton rack, advertising 25¢ cartons, sign has French on one side and English on the reverse side, 1930s, 5' tall, EX ....$475.00 D

Metal, golf hole, 1950s, EX......$25.00 C

Porcelain, "Drink Coke," "Ask for it either way," 1940s, 9" dia., EX, $375.00 C. Courtesy of Mitchell collection.

Porcelain, double-sided prescription sign, with metal hanger, "Made in U.S.A 1933, Tenn. Enamel Mfg. Co., Nash," designed to hang over sidewalk from building arm, white & yellow lettering on red & green, 60½" x 46½", 1933, EX, $1,200.00 B. Courtesy of Collectors Auction Services.

Porcelain, double-sided hanging sign, with additional bottle sign that gives a 3-D effect, designed to hang from store arm over sidewalk, white on red, 48" x 60", 1923, G, $625.00 B. Courtesy of Collectors Auction Services.

Metal "Have a Coke" with spotlight bottle in a metal frame, 1940s, 18" x 54", EX ....$325.00 D.

Metal, "Ice Cold" with cup in center, 1960s, 20" x 28", NM .... $300.00 B

Metal light-up sign, "Drink Coca-Cola" on disc, wall basket, 1950s, EX ....$300.00 C

Metal lollipop sign "Drink Coca-Cola refresh!," 1940 – 1950s, F .... $595.00 D

Metal, painted "Drink Coca-Cola ... Sold Here Ice Cold," rolled self frame, has Christmas bottle in center, 1932, EX ....$695.00 D

Metal, painted "Drink ..." sign with bottle in spotlight, 1948, 54" x 18", G... $350.00 D

Metal, painted sign with rolled edge, "Enjoy Coke ... Have a Coke and a smile ... Coke adds life," white, red, and black, 1960 – 1970s, EX...$125.00 D

Metal, "Pause Refresh yourself," various scenes in yellow border, lettering, 1950s, 28" x 10", VG.............$235.00 C

Porcelain, double-sided with mounting hanger advertising tourist shop and Coca-Cola, Coke sign is mounted to bottom which gives a 3-D effect, 40" x 58", VG, $1,400.00 B. Courtesy of Collectors Auction Services.

Porcelain, self framing, single sided sign, "Tenn. Enamel Manufacturing Co. Nashville," advertising fountain service, yellow, red, white on green, 60" x 45½", EX, $2,200.00 B. Courtesy of Collectors Auction Services.

Porcelain, French Canadian flange sign, "Buvez Coca-Cola Glace," 1950s, 18" x 19", NM, $225.00 D. Courtesy of Muddy River Trading Co./Gary Metz.

Metal pilaster sign with graphics of 12 pack and the message "pick up 12" with original connecting material and button at top, 1954, 16" x 55", NM ....$3,300.00 B

Metal policeman crossing guard with original base. This is a very volatile piece. I've seen them sell for as little as $600.00 or as high as $3,500.00. 1950s, G...$1,300.00 D

Metal rack, round, "Take home a Carton," 1930 – 1940s, EX .... $200.00 C

Metal rolled frame edge, "Coke adds life to everything nice" with dynamic wave, 1960s, EX ....$275.00 D

Metal rolled frame edge with "Pick up 12... Refreshment for All," with artwork of 12 pack carton, 1960s, 50" x 16", EX ....$550.00 D

Metal, sidewalk, "For Headache and Exhaustion Drink Coca-Cola," with 4" legs, manufactured by Ronemers & Co, Baltimore, Md., 1895 – 90, G...$7,500.00 B

Metal sign with rolled framing edge, "Things go better with Coke," bottle at right of message, 35¼" x 35¼", G...$275.00 D

Porcelain, outdoor bottle, tall vertical, "Drink Coca-Cola," believed to be a foreign sign where English was the dominant language, 1950 – 1960s, 16" x 4', NM, $475.00 D. Courtesy of Muddy River Trading Co./Gary Metz.

Porcelain foreign sign, 1950s – 60s, 18" x 24", EX, $225.00 B. Courtesy of Muddy River Trading Co./Gary Metz.

Porcelain, horizontal, "Drink Coca-Cola Fountain Service," yellow background, 1950s, 28" x 12", $700.00 B. Courtesy of Muddy River Trading Co./Gary Metz.

Metal string holder with double-sided panels, "Take Home Coca-Cola in Cartons," featured with six pack for 25¢, 1930s, EX ....$1,100.00 B

Metal Tab self-framing sign with the message "flavor in — calories out", 31½" x 12", VG .... $265.00 C

Metal whirly top with original base with four wings and eight sides for advertisement, NOS, 1950, NM ....$750.00 C

Neon, "Coca-Cola in bottles," great colors with metal base, 1950s, EX .... $3,000.00 D

Neon, "Coke with Ice," three colors, 1980s, EX...............................$425.00 D

Neon sign with original wrinkle paint, 1939, 17" x 13½", G ....$1,700.00 B

Oil cloth, Lillian Nordica, "Coca-Cola at Soda Fountain 5¢ Delicious Refreshing," rare, 1904, 25" x 47", EX ....$13,000.00 C

Oil on canvas that has been dry mounted on board, featuring soda jerk with glasses of Coke, back is marked Forbes Litho, 1940s, 22" x 17", F ....$2,300.00 B

Original artwork of outdoor retail location, 1970s, 30" x 20", EX ..... $150.00 C

Porcelain, flange, "Refresh Yourself, Coca-Cola Sold Here Ice Cold" on shield shaped sign, 1930s, 17" x 20", G, $525.00 B. Courtesy of Muddy River Trading Co./Gary Metz.

Porcelain, double-sided flange sign, "Drink Coca-Cola Here," 1940s, NM, $850.00 B. Courtesy of Muddy River Trading Co./Gary Metz.

Porcelain fountain service sign with red stripes on white background and button at right of message, 1950s, 30" x 12", G, $325.00 B. Courtesy of Muddy River Trading Co./Gary Metz.

Paper advertising, "See adventures of Kit Carson," 1953, 24" x 16", EX ....$135.00 C

Paper, calendar print sent to bottlers in advance of calendar, two models on a beach outing, framed under glass, rare, 1917, NM .... $8,200.00 C

Paper, "Drink Coca-Cola Delicious and Refreshing," bottle in front of hot dog, framed and under glass, EX ....$175.00 C

Paper, "Drink Coca-Cola, Quick Refreshment," bottle in front of hot dog, framed under glass, EX .... $175.00 C

Paper, Edgar Bergen and Charlie McCarthy, CBS Sunday Evenings, 1949, 22" x 11", EX ....$200.00 C

Paper, Gibson Girl, matted and framed, if in mint condition price would go to about $5,000.00, 1910, 20" x 30", EX ....$4,500.00 C

Paper, girl in white dress with large red bow in back with a bottle and a straw, matted and framed under glass. There are two versions of this, the other one is identical except the waist bow is pink. 1910s, F............................. $3,800.00 C

Porcelain, side-walk sign and legs, double-sided, "Stop Here Drink Coca-Cola," 1941, 27" x 46", VG, $850.00 C. Courtesy of Muddy River Trading Co./Gary Metz.

Porcelain flange, die cut, "Rafraichissez vous Coca-Cola," foreign, VG, $425.00 C.

Porcelain one-sided neon, "Drug Store... Fountain Service", 86" x 58" x 8", G, $3,500.00 B. Courtesy of Collectors Auction Services.

Paper, Lupe Velez in swim suit holding a bottle, framed and under glass, 1932, 11" x 21½", NM..................$1,250.00 C

Paper poster featuring man and woman with flared glasses and the globe motif, 1912, 38" x 49", F............ $16,500.00 B

Paper poster, horizontal, "Let's have a Coke," couple in uniform, 1930s, 57" x 20", G.....................................$850.00 B

Paper poster, horizontal, "Such a friendly custom," two women in uniform at soda fountain, 1930s, G.........$375.00 C

Paper poster "Refresh," on heavy outdoor paper, 1940s, 57" x 18", EX ....$300.00 D

Paper poster, "Ritz Boy," first time Ritz Boy was used, framed under glass, 1920s, F..................................$700.00 C

Paper, poster, "The Taste You're Thirsty For," featuring a large cup of Coke, Diet Coke, and, of course, Sprite, 24" x 18", 1985, NM ....$25.00 C

Tin, *"Beverages" with 12" buttons on each end, hard to find sign, 70" x 12", 1950s, EX, $950.00 B. Courtesy of Muddy River Trading Co./Gary Metz.*

Stainless steel from dispenser, "Drink Coca-Cola," horizontal lettering, 1930s, 6½" x 3¼", G, $95.00 D. Courtesy of Gary Metz.

Reverse glass with original chain and frame, "Drink Coca-Cola," rare version in red, white lettering on red background, 1932, 20" x 12", EX, $3,500.00 B. Courtesy of Muddy River Trading Co./Gary Metz.

Paper poster, vertical, "Pause a minute Refresh yourself," roll down with top and bottom metal strips, 1927 – 1928, 12" x 20", EX ....$1,800.00 B

Paper, "That taste-good feeling," boy with Coca-Cola and hot dog, 1920s, F ....$200.00 D

Paper, "Take Along Coke In 12 oz. Cans, Buy A Case," men beside boat, 1960s, 35" x 19", EX ....$150.00 D

Paper, "That Taste-Good Feeling," 1920s, 14" x 20", VG.............$300.00 D

Paper, "Treat Yourself Right, Drink Coca-Cola," 1920s, 12" x 20", VG.. $675.00 B

Paper, "which" Coca-Cola or Goldelle Ginger Ale, 1905, VG.........$5,000.00 D

Paper, window set for bottle sales, three-piece, "Home Refreshment," 1941, 31" tall, EX ....$350.00 D

Paper, window sign, "Let Us Put A Case In Your Car," case of Coca-Cola, 36" x 20", EX ....$300.00 D

Pennant with the message "Enjoy Coke We're #1," EX ....$15.00 C

Tin, bottle, oval, "Drink A Bottle of Carbonated Coca-Cola," rare, 1900s, 8½" x 10½", G, $6,000.00 C.

Tin bottle rack sign with space for price for "Big King size," 1960s, 9" x 17", EX, $125.00 B. Courtesy of Muddy River Trading Co./Gary Metz.

Tin, bottle, Christmas, 1933, 3' tall, EX, $1,000.00 C.

Pennant with the message "Taste Diet Coke," EX .... $15.00 C

Plastic and metal, light-up die cut sign, shaped like a paper serving cup, 1950 – 60s, 16" x 17", G.................$1,300.00 D

Plastic, "Delicious With Ice Cold Coca-Cola," popcorn box overflowing with popcorn, 24" x 7", G ....$50.00 D

Plastic, "Delicious With Ice Cold Coca-Cola," popcorn box overflowing with popcorn, 24" x 7", EX..............$65.00 D

Plastic front, light-up sign that gives a movement illusion when lit, "Drink Coca-Cola In Bottles" in red center, 1960s, 11" dia., EX ....$725.00 D

Plastic, "Here's the real thing, Coke," wave logo, 1970s, 51" x 7", M ..$30.00 D

Plastic, light-up, "Work Safely," "Safety is a job" cardboard insert, shows a Coca-Cola paper cup in lower left, 1950s, 15½" sq., EX ....$725.00 D

Plywood and metal Kay Displays advertising "Pause Here," yellow, red, and black, 37" x 10", 1930s, G...$1,550.00 B

Tin button featuring decal of six pack "Standard 6," 1950s, 16" dia., NM, $425.00 B. Courtesy of Muddy River Trading Co./Gary Metz.

Tin button sign with the original applied decal featuring two different size bottles and the price on each, 1950s, 16" dia., NM, $450.00 B. Courtesy of Muddy River Trading Co./ Gary Metz.

Tin, carton rack with great rare sign at top, hard to find this one, 1930s, 5' tall, NM, $825.00 B. Courtesy of Muddy River Trading Co./Gary Metz.

Plywood and metal, Kay Displays sign, black lettering on yellow background, 1930s, 37" x 10", G.............$1,550.00 D

Plywood, double sided, "Slow School Zone Enjoy Coca-Cola, Drive Safely," 1950 – 1960s, EX...................$950.00 C

Plywood, soda person with a glass of Coke, center part of festoon, 1930 – 1940s, EX.............................$375.00 B

Plywood, triangle die-cut sign with down arrow, "Ice Cold Drink Coca-Cola," Kay Displays, 1933, EX ....$575.00 B

Porcelain button sign, "Drink Coca-Cola in Bottles," white on red, 2' dia., NM ....$425.00 B

Porcelain, Canadian fountain service sign, 1935, 27" x 14", NM .... $1,300.00 D

Porcelain, "Delicious, Refreshing" with bottle in center, 1950s, 24" square, EX .... $250.00 D

Porcelain double-sided dispenser sign with metal frame, 28" x 27", G...$850.00 B

Tin, Canadian sign featuring 6 oz. bottle on right, 1930s, 28" x 20", G, $350.00 C. Courtesy of Muddy River Trading Co./Gary Metz.

Tin, Canadian, six pack in spotlight "Take home a carton," 1940, 36" x 60", G, $250.00 C.

Tin, button, white painted with bottle in center, 1940s, 24" dia., NM, rare and hard to find, $400.00 B. Courtesy of Muddy River Trading Co./ Gary Metz.

Porcelain, double-sided flange sign, "Drink Coca-Cola Here," 1940s, NM ....$850.00 B

Porcelain, double-sided fountain sign, featuring an early dispenser, 25" x 26", 1941, EX ....$2,200.00 B

Porcelain, double-sided hanging sign, with additional bottle sign that gives a 3-D effect, designed to hang from store arm over sidewalk, white on red, 48" x 60", 1923, G .... $625.00 B

Porcelain, double-sided lunch sign, 1950s, 28" x 25", NM ....$1,500.00 B

Porcelain, double-sided prescriptions sign, with metal hanger, "Made in U.S.A 1933, Tenn. Enamel Mfg. Co., Nash," designed to hang over sidewalk from building arm, white and yellow lettering on red and green, 60½" x 46½", 1933, G....................... $595.00 C

Porcelain double-sided sidewalk sign with bracket for hanging over sidewalk on arm, featuring a courtesy panel at top with Coke bottle at bottom in yellow spotlight, 5' x 5', VG ....$850.00 B

Tin, die-cut fishtail, with turned edges, "Coca-Cola," white or red, 26" x 12", 1962, NM, $200.00 B. Courtesy of Muddy River Trading Co./Gary Metz.

Tin, double-sided flange sign with arrow shape at bottom, carrying the message "lunch," 1950, 18" x 22", NM, $4,000.00 B. Courtesy of Muddy River Trading Co./Gary Metz.

Tin, double-sided rack sign, "Take Home a Carton ... Coca-Cola ... 6 bottles 25¢ plus deposit," yellow and white on red, 13" dia., 1930s, G, $225.00 C.

Porcelain, double-sided with mounting hanger advertising tourist shop and Coca-Cola, Coke sign is mounted to bottom which gives a 3-D effect, 40" x 58", G.....................................$795.00 D

Porcelain, fishtail sign with turned ends, "Drink Coca-Cola," white on red, 1950s, 44" x 16", M................$325.00 B

Porcelain, flange, "Enjoy Coca-Cola In bottles," very rare, 1948, EX....$950.00 D

Porcelain, flange mount, "Iced Coca-Cola Here," yellow and white lettering on red background with yellow trim around outside of sign, 1950s, NM..$750.00 C

Porcelain, fountain service, diagonal, "Drink Coca-Cola," 1933, 22" x 26", NM.....................................$1,100.00 C

Porcelain, fountain service, "Drink Coca-Cola Fountain Service," white and yellow lettering on red and black background framed by fountain heads, 27" x 14", EX..............................$1,200.00 D

Tin, "Drink Coca-Cola Enjoy that Refreshing New Feeling," painted fishtail with Coca-Cola bottle on right side, 1960s, 32" x 12", VG, $235.00 D.

Tin dynamic wave sign, unusual variation, 1970s, 35" x 13", EX, $125.00 B. Courtesy of Muddy River Trading Co./Gary Metz.

Tin, "Enjoy Coca-Cola Ice Cold" with message at top and graphics of bottle at bottom, 1960s, 18" x 54", G, $210.00 B. Courtesy of Muddy River Trading Co./Gary Metz.

Porcelain, fountain service sign, "Fountain Service, Drink Coca-Cola," red, green, white, 1950s, 28" x 12", EX ....$800.00 D

Porcelain, fountain service, two-sided, dispenser with stainless steel banding around the edge of the sign, 1950s, 27" x 28", VG ....$375.00 C

Porcelain, French Canadian sign, because of its construction it resembles the smaller door push, 1930s, 18" x 54", G..$400.00 B

Porcelain, horizontal, "Coca-Cola Sold Here Ice Cold," red background trimmed in yellow with white lettering, 1940s, 29" x 12", EX .... $275.00 D

Porcelain, horizontal, "Coca-Cola Sold Here Ice Cold," red background trimmed in yellow with white lettering, 1940s, 29" x 12", EX ....$375.00 C

Porcelain, Italian sign with button inside square, NOS, white on red, 22" square, EX............................. $225.00 B

Tin, featuring Elaine holding a glass, 1916, 20" x 30", VG, $5,700.00 C.

Tin, embossed, "Drink Coca-Cola Delicious and Refreshing," 14" x 10", F, $225.00 C. *Courtesy of Gary Metz.*

Tin, embossed "Drink Coca-Cola Delicious and Refreshing" with bottle at left of message, with trademark in tail, 1930s, 36" x 12", EX, $550.00 C. *Courtesy of Mitchell collection.*

Porcelain, kick plate for screen door, "Drink Coca-Cola Sold Here Ice Cold," 1930s, 31" x 12", G ....$475.00 C

Porcelain, outdoor advertising sign, "Drug Store, Drink Coca-Cola, Delicious and Refreshing," red, white, and green, 1933, 5' x 3½', EX ....$1,500.00 D

Porcelain outdoor bottle, tall vertical, "Drink Coca-Cola," believed to be a foreign sign where English was the dominant language, 1950 – 1960s, 16" x 4', NM ....$475.00 D

Porcelain, outdoor, "Drink Coca-Cola Delicious and Refreshing," white and yellow lettering on red background, 1938, 8' x 4', NM.................$1,300.00 D

Porcelain, shield sign, "Drink Coca-Cola," white, yellow, and red, 36" x 24", 1942, EX........................, $325.00 B

Porcelain, sidewalk, double-sided, courtesy panel over a 24" button, NOS, 1950s, 2' x 5', EX ....$3,200.00 B

Porcelain, sidewalk sign and legs, double sided, "Stop Here Drink Coca-Cola," 1941, 27" x 46", VG ....$850.00 C

Tin, embossed painted Spanish kick plate, message is in center between straight-sided bottles, 36" x 12", 1908, EX, $2,300.00 B. Courtesy of Muddy River Trading Co./Gary Metz.

Tin, embossed painted kick plate featuring the 1923 bottle, white on red, 35" x 11", 1933, EX, $900.00 B. Courtesy of Muddy River Trading Co./Gary Metz.

Tin embossed sign with 1923 bottle "Delicious and refreshing," 54" x 30", 1934, EX, $525.00 B. Courtesy of Muddy River Trading Co./Gary Metz.

Porcelain, single-sided sign, French, yellow and white lettering on red, 30½" x 12", EX................................$200.00 B

Porcelain truck cab sign with the message "Drink Coca-Cola Ice Cold," 1950s, 50" x 10", EX ....$350.00 B

Reverse glass, "Drink Coca-Cola," for back bar mirror, 1930s, 11" dia., VG....................................$625.00 C

Reverse glass, "Drink Coca-Cola," 1920s, 10" x 6", EX ....$1,250.00 C

Reverse glass with original chain and frame, "Drink Coca-Cola," rare version in red, white lettering on red background, 1932, 20" x 12", EX .... $3,500.00 B

Sticker, "Please Pay Cashier," 1960s, EX .... $25.00 C

Sticker, "Please Pay Cashier," 13" x 6", 1960s, EX................................. $5.00 C

Tin, "Beverages" with 12" buttons on each end, hard-to-find sign, 70" x 12", 1950s, EX..............................$950.00 B

Tin, Hilda Clark, round, "Coca-Cola Drink Delicious and Refreshing," very rare and hard-to-find piece, 1903, 6" dia., EX, $5,700.00 C.

Tin, flange, "Drink Coca-Cola" with bottle in spotlight at lower corner, 1947, 24" x 20", G, $575.00 D. Courtesy of Rare Bird Antique Mall.

Tin bottle, embossed, 1931, 4½" x 12½", VG.............................$375.00 B

Tin button sign with bottle in hand decal, 1950s, 16" dia., NM.....$250.00 B

Tin button with painted message "Drink Coca-Cola ... Sign of Good Taste," white and yellow lettering on red, 16", 1948, EX .... $450.00 C

Tin Canadian sign "Drink Coca-Cola" with bottle, 1959, G............... $300.00 B

Tin, carton rack with great rare sign at top, hard to find this one, 1930s, 5' tall, VG.. $495.00 C

Tin distributors, oval, from McRae Coca-Cola Bottling Co. in Helena, Georgia, featuring pretty long-haired girl, 1910, EX.....................$3,500.00 D

Tin, double-sided die cut arrow flange, "Drink Coca-Cola Ice Cold," with button at top and bottle in lower arrow point, EX............................... $550.00 D

Tin fishtail sign with message panel "Candy-Cigarettes," 1960s, EX, $300.00 B. Courtesy of Muddy River Trading Co./Gary Metz.

Tin "Ice Cold...Prepared by the bottler of Coca-Cola" sign in the vertical version with graphics of '60s cup, 1960s, 20" x 28", EX, $550.00 B. Courtesy of Muddy River Trading Co./ Gary Metz.

Tin, double-sided die cut arrow sign "Ice Cold Coca-Cola Sold Here," 1927, 30" x 8", VG..........................$400.00 C Beware of reproductions.

Tin, double-sided flange fishtail sign, red on white and green, 1960s, 18" x 15", VG ....$325.00 C

Tin, double-sided rack sign, "Take Home a Carton ... Coca-Cola ... 6 bottles 25¢ plus deposit," yellow and white on red, 13" dia., 1930s, EX .... $395.00 C

Tin, double-sided tire sign, "Enjoy Coca-Cola," 17" dia., 1952, EX ....$3,400.00 B

Tin, "Drink Coca-Cola" button with silver metal arrow, 1950 – 1960s, 18" dia., VG..$750.00 C

Tin, "Drink Coca-Cola" sign with marching bottles, note shadow on bottles, 1937, 54" x 18", NM ..... $800.00 B

Tin, "Drink Coca-Cola," 24" iron frame, one side has a 16" button while the opposite side has a 10" plastic button with a small light which creates a back light, VG............................. $1,050.00 C

Tin, self framing, new Betty, "Drink Coca-Cola" sign, yellow and white on red, 1940, 28" x 20", G, $250.00 C. Courtesy of Muddy River Trading Co./ Gary Metz.

Tin, self framing, horizontal oval, "Coca-Cola," girl in foreground offering a bottle, 1926, 11" x 8", VG, $950.00 D.

Tin, "Drink Coca-Cola," with couple at right of message holding bottle, 1940s, 35" x 11", EX..........................$575.00 D

Tin, embossed, Buvez Coca-Cola, painted, foreign, 17¼" x 53", G..$125.00 C

Tin, embossed "Gas Today," with bottle in hand, red, white, and yellow, 23½" x 15", 1926, G...........................$775.00 B

Tin, embossed over cardboard with string holder, "Drink Coca-Cola," 1922, 8" x 4", EX.............................$900.00 B

Tin, embossed painted kick plate, white and yellow lettering on red, 27" x 10", 1931, EX ....$750.00 B

Tin, embossed painted sign with border and straight line advertising, red, yellow, and white, 20" dia., 1932, NM .... $1,250.00 B

Tin, embossed painted Spanish kick plate, message is in center between straight- sided bottles, 36" x 12", 1908, EX ....$2,300.00 B

Tin, painted, "Drink Coca-Cola," shoulders and head of girl drinking from a bottle, yellow and white lettering on red background, self-framing, 1940, 34" x 12", EX, $475.00 D. *Courtesy of Muddy River Trading Co./Gary Metz.*

Tin over cardboard with beveled edge, for China use, rare, 11" x 8", EX, $675.00 C. *Courtesy of Bill Mitchell.*

Tin, sidewalk insert sign with the message "Big King Size" and graphics of large bottle and fishtail logo at top, 1960s, 20" x 28", EX, $450.00 B. *Courtesy of Muddy River Trading Co./Gary Metz.*

Tin, flange, "Drink Coca-Cola" with bottle in spotlight at lower corner, 1947, 24" x 20", G .... $575.00 D

Tin, flat "Refresh yourself" sign "Drink Coca-Cola Sold Here Ice Cold," yellow and white on red, 1927, 28" x 29", VG... $450.00 D

Tin, Hilda Clark, showing her drinking from a glass while seated at a table with roses and stationery, very rare, 1899, VG................................... $15,500.00 C

Tin, horizontal, "Drink Coca-Cola," self framing, white, VG, 32" x 10½", 1927, VG..$750.00 D

Tin, horizontal embossed, "Drink Coca-Cola Ice Cold," matted and framed, white and yellow lettering on red and black background, bottle in left part of sign, 1936, 28" x 20", EX ..... $850.00 C

Tin, "Ice Cold Coca-Cola Sold Here," yellow and white on red, 1933, 20" dia., G...$225.00 B

Tin, "Ice Cold" sign featuring artwork of '60s cup of Coke, white lettering on blue background, 28" x 20", 1960s, NM .... $675.00 B

Tin, self-framing fishtail logo sign with diamond can on left and bottle at right with advertising for "Delicatessen" at top, 1960s, 5' x 2', EX, $650.00 B. Courtesy of Muddy River Trading Co./Gary Metz.

Tin, shadow bottle "Ice Cold" sign, hard to find, 1936, 18" x 54", G, $600.00 B. Courtesy of Muddy River Trading Co./ Gary Metz.

Tin, sign advertising "Home Cooking Served with a Coke," Fay's Cafe, 1950s, 50" x 16", EX, $300.00 B. Courtesy of Muddy River Trading Co./Gary Metz.

Tin, Lillian Nordica, self framed, embossed, promoting both fountain and bottle sales, 1904 – 1905, EX .... $8,500.00 C

Tin, "Now! Enjoy Coca-Cola at home," featuring hand carrying cardboard six pack, rare and hard to find, Canadian sign, 1930s, 18" x 54", F.... $1,050.00 B

Tin, outdoor sign, courtesy panel blank, 72" x 36", 1950 – 1960s, F...... $95.00 C

Tin over cardboard, "Drink Coca-Cola," with bottle graphics, 1920s, 6" x 13", VG.....................................$1,200.00 B

Tin over cardboard with beveled edge, for use in China, rare, 11" x 8", EX .... $675.00 C

Tin, painted, "Drink Coca-Cola," shoulders and head of girl drinking from a bottle, yellow and white lettering on red background, self framing, 1940, 34" x 12", EX ....$475.00 D

Tin, painted, "Take a case home today $1.00 plus deposit," 19½" x 27¾", VG....................................... $235.00 C

Tin, sign "Things go better with Coke," with bottle at bottom, 18" x 54", 1960s, NM, $475.00 B.Courtesy of Muddy River Trading Co./ Gary Metz.

Tin, sidewalk sign featuring graphics of the fishtail logo at top with a six pack at bottom, "Take home a carton," 1959, 20" x 28", NM, $950.00 B.Courtesy of Muddy River Trading Co./Gary Metz.

Tin, sign "Things go better with Coke" and graphics of hob-bleskirt bottle, 1960s, 3' square, EX, $300.00 B.Courtesy of Muddy River Trading Co./Gary Metz.

Tin, painted vertical, self-framing, "Drink Coca-Cola, Take home a carton," with spotlighted early six pack, "Made in Canada 1942 by St. Thomas Metal Signs Ltd," white and yellow on red, 17" x 53½", 1942, EX ....$750.00 B

Tin, painted vertical sign, message "Take Home a Carton" at top over cardboard carton 6 for 25¢ in yellow spotlight over the message "Drink Coca-Cola" at bottom, 1930s, 18" x 54", G .... $250.00 B

Tin, "Pause ... Drink Coca-Cola," considered to be rare due to the 1939 – 1940 cooler in the left-hand spotlight, all on red back ground, horizontal lettering, self framing, 1940, 42" x 18", EX .... $2,400.00 B

Tin, "Pause" sign with bottle in spotlight, 1940, 18" x 54", VG..$775.00 B

Tin, pilaster sign, rare version with the message "Refresh Yourself," under button, 16" x 52", 1950, EX ....$1,400.00 B

Tin, sign, "Things go Better," featuring "Drink" paper cup, hard to find, red, green, and white, 1960s, 28" x 20", NM, $600.00 B. Courtesy of Muddy River Trading Co./Gary Metz.

Tin 12-pack die-cut sign in likeness of 12-pack carton, 1954, NM, $3,000.00 B. Courtesy of Muddy River Trading Co./Gary Metz.

Tin, strip tacker type sign with "Drink Coca-Cola in bottles 5¢," 1922, 23½" x 6", NM, $1,350.00 B. Courtesy of Muddy River Trading Co./Gary Metz.

Tin, pilaster sign that advertises "Serve Coke at Home" with graphics of 25¢ six pack, original button with all connecting hardware, 1940s – 50s, 16" x 55", EX ....$900.00 B

Tin, pilaster sign with plain "Drink Coca-Cola" button at top and plain bottle at center of the sign, 1948, EX .... $625.00 B

Tin, pilaster sign with the "Drink Coca-Cola" button at sign top and graphics of 1950s six pack, 1950s, NM .... $700.00 B

Tin, rack sign, "Take Home a carton 6 bottles 25¢," 18" x 9", 1930s, EX ...$225.00 C

Tin, self-framed "Luncheonette" sign with advertising for both a bottle and a can with a fishtail "Coca-Cola," 59¼" x 23¼", EX ....$375.00 C

Tin, sidewalk insert sign with the message "things go better with Coke," 1960s, 20" x 28", VG ....$500.00 B

Tin, sidewalk sign featuring 24 bottle case "Take a case home today," 1957, EX .... $250.00 D

Tin, sign, "Coca-Cola with soda 5¢," a very rare sign and possibly one of a kind, manufactured by Tuchfarber Co., Cincinnati, 17" x 12", 1902, G ....$7,200.00 B

65

Tin, "turtle" sign, so called because of the shape, "Drink Coca-Cola The Delicious Beverage," 1920s, 20" x 15", G, $1,800.00 B. *Courtesy of Muddy River Trading Co./Gary Metz.*

Tin, "Take Home a carton," self framing border, Canadian, 1950, 35" x 53", $625.00 B. *Courtesy of Muddy River Trading Co./Gary Metz.*

Wood and bent metal, carries the message "Drink Coca-Cola ... Please pay when served." This is an unusual double-sided flange sign, 1940 – 50s, 15" x 12", EX, $1,250.00 B. *Courtesy of Muddy River Trading Co./Gary Metz.*

Tin, sign, "Enjoy Big King Size" over fishtail with bottle at right, 56" x 32", 1960s, EX .... $375.00 B

Tin, sign, "Enjoy that Refreshing new Feeling" with fishtail logo and bottle, 56" x 32", 1960s, EX ....$300.00 B

Tin, sign, "Things go Better," featuring "Drink" paper cup, hard to find, red, green, and white, 1960s, 28" x 20", NM .... $600.00 B

Tin, sign, "Things go better with Coke" with a courtesy panel at top and graphics of bottle at right of sign, 1960s, 5' x 3', G ....$275.00 B

Tin, sign with bottle and the message "5¢ ice cold," 1936 EX ....$2,700.00 B

Tin, sign with decal of bottle, 16" x 50", 1940 – 1950s, EX.................. $425.00 B

Tin, sign with rolled edge, "Enjoy Big King Size ... Ice Cold Here," fishtail design, 1960s, 28" x 20", G..$250.00 D

Tin, sign with screen printed bottle in hand, "delicious and refreshing," most of these bottle in hand images are decals, 1954, 18" x 54", EX .... $2,100.00 B

Wood arrow, "Drink Coca-Cola Ice Cold," silver painted bottle and arrow, 17" dia., F, $500.00 D. Courtesy of Gary Metz.

Wood composition Kay Displays medallion sign with the message "Please pay cashier" and a likeness of a glass on the top center, 1940s, 13" dia., EX, $950.00 B.

Wood, Kay Displays sign with "Pause" top line and "Drink Coca-Cola" and on last line is "Refresh," 1940s, 14" x 10½", EX, $2,900.00 B. Courtesy of Muddy River Trading Co./Gary Metz.

Tin, six pack die cut sign, featuring carrier with handle, advertising 6 for 25¢, 1950, 11" x 13", EX ....$775.00 B

Tin, six pack, embossed die cut, featuring a King Size six pack, 1963, 3' x 2½', EX........................... $700.00 B

Tin, six pack, embossed die cut, 1963, 3' x 2½', EX...........................$725.00 B

Trolley car sign with graphics of a couple presenting a toast with Coke in glasses, 1927, 21" x 11", EX ....$3,000.00 B

Trolley car sign with graphics of pretty young girl with a bottle of Coke, "Absolutely Sanitary," very rare item, 1912, 21" x 11", F .... $2,300.00 B

Trolley car sign with the ladies known as the four seasons, "Drink Coca-Cola delicious and refreshing all the year round," framed and matted which has cut the overall size of the sign down, it was probably originally 21" x 11", 1923, 19½" x 9¾", EX ...... $3,200.00 B

Wire and tin, "Wherever you go," tropical island, 1960s, 14" x 18", EX .....$215.00 C

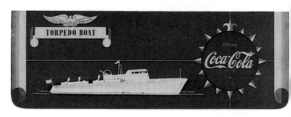

Wood and masonite, torpedo boat sign, 1940s, EX, $335.00 C. Courtesy of Mitchell collection.

Wood, Kay Displays, "Lunch with us ... a tasty sandwich with Coca-Cola," difficult to find, 1940s, 9" x 13", EX, $2,900.00 B. Courtesy of Muddy River Trading Co./Gary Metz.

Wood, Kay Displays with metal filigree, center graphics of marching Coke glasses, 1940, 9" x 11", EX, $525.00 B. Courtesy of Muddy River Trading Co./Gary Metz.

Wood finish with chrome accents "Thirst asks nothing more," difficult to locate this piece, 38" x 10", G, $775.00 B. Courtesy of Muddy River Trading Co./Gary Metz.

Wire and wood, Kay Displays sign with bowling scene, 1940s, 16" dia., EX .... $425.00 B

Wood finish with chrome accents "Thirst asks nothing more," difficult to locate this piece, 38" x 10", G...$775.00 B

Wood, hand-painted, truck sign, double-sided with the maker's name on one side, with original metal brackets, "Every Bottle Sterilized," white lettering on red background, 1920s, 10' x 1', F ....$450.00 D

Wood, Silhouette Girl, metal hanger, 1940, VG..............................$225.00 C

Wood, Silhouette Girl, metal hanger, 1940, EX, $475.00 C. Courtesy of Mitchell collection.

"Drink Coca-Cola," brass perpetual desk, VG, $165.00 C. Courtesy of Mitchell collection.

Bamboo calendar top from the Coca-Cola Bottler in Herrin, Illinois, with super graphics of the sun, low in the sky and a Japanese building in front of a mountain, extremely difficult to locate, 1920s, VG, $250.00 C. Courtesy of Al and Earlene Mitchell.

Perpetual desk, showing day, month, and year, 1920, EX, $385.00 C.

Calendar top, featuring Hilda Clark, 7⅝" x 6", 1901, EX.............$3,900.00 B

Calendar top, missing the bottom pad area, 1909, 11" x 14", EX......$5,500.00 B

Calendar with fishtail top and replaceable bottom tear sheets, 1960s, EX .... $475.00 B

"Drink Coca-Cola," brass perpetual desk, M.................................$300.00 C

"Drink Coca-Cola," brass perpetual desk, F .... $75.00 C

Paper, Jim Harrison calendar with that wonderful front page of the old lunch store, 1999, M ....$10.00 C

Perpetual desk, showing day, month, and year, 1920, G .... $225.00 C

Tin, calendar holder with daily tear sheets at bottom featuring tin button at top, red and white, 1950s, 8" x 19", EX .... $415.00 D

Tin, fishtail calendar holder with daily tear sheets at bottom red and white, 1960s, 9" x 13", NM .... $175.00 C

1906, Juanita, "Drink Coca-Cola Delicious Refreshing," framed, matted, under glass, 7" x 15", $5,000.00 D.

Bamboo calendar top from the Coca-Cola Bottler in Herrin, Illinois, minus tear sheets, strong graphics of mountain scene and small village on water, difficult to locate good examples of this item, VG, $250.00 C. Courtesy of Al and Earlene Mitchell.

Calendar with one original tear sheet, 7" x 14", 1908, EX, $7,200.00 B. Courtesy of Muddy River Trading Co./ Gary Metz.

1891, from Asa Chandler & Co., featuring girl in period dress holding sport racquet with full pad moved to reveal full face of sheet, rare, EX.........$10,500.00 B

1897, "Coca-Cola at all Soda Fountains," all monthly pads displayed at once, 7" x 12", EX .... $10,000.00 C

1901, "Drink Coca-Cola at all Soda Fountains 5¢" with full monthly pad, framed, matted, and under glass, rare, EX .... $5,500.00 C

1902, "Drink Coca-Cola 5¢" with wrong month sheet, EX...... $5,500.00 C

1904, Lillian Nordica standing by table with a glass, 7" x 15", F.....$2,400.00 D

1906, Juanita, "Drink Coca-Cola Delicious Refreshing," framed, matted, under glass, 7" x 15", EX... $5,000.00 D

1907, "Drink Coca-Cola Delicious Refreshing, Relieves Fatigue, Sold Everywhere 5¢," G ....$2,500.00 D

1907, "Drink Coca-Cola Delicious Refreshing, Relieves Fatigue Sold Everywhere 5¢" featuring woman in period dress holding up a glass of Coca-Cola, EX............................. $6,000.00 C

1915, Elaine, matted and framed with partial pad, VG, $1,450.00 C. Courtesy of Muddy River Trading Co./Gary Metz.

Original Betty calendar with the very scarce bottle version, has one original tear sheet, 1914, EX, $3,300.00 B. *Courtesy of Muddy River Trading Co./Gary Metz.*

1916, Elaine with bottle, partial pad, under glass in frame, 13" x 32", M, $2,000.00 C. Courtesy of Mitchell collection.

1911, the Coca-Cola Girl, "Drink Delicious Coca-Cola," framed under glass, 10" x 17", Hamilton King, M... $4,600.00 B

1913, top, girl in white hat with red ribbon, value would double if complete, rare piece matted and framed under glass, EX ....$4,000.00 C

1914, Betty, full pad and original metal strip at top, VG....................$1,450.00 C

1916, Elaine with glass, pad, 13" x 32", M...$1,600.00 D

1916, World War I Girl holding a glass, she also appears holding a bottle of another version, framed, 13" x 32", G...$1,200.00 C

1917, Constance, with glass, full pad, matted and framed under glass, VG.....................................$1,750.00 C

1918, June Caprice with glass, framed under glass, VG.....................$275.00 C

1919, Knitting Girl, great artwork of girl with bottle and a knitting bag, full pad, 13" x 32", EX ....$3,500.00 C

1929, flapper girl in green dress with string of beads displaying both glass and bottle, full pad, framed under glass, 12" x 24", M, $1,025.00 C.
Courtesy of Mitchell collection.

1917, Constance, with glass, full pad, framed and matted under glass, EX, $2,550.00 C.
Courtesy of Mitchell collection.

1931, boy at fishing hole with dog, sandwich, and a bottle, full pad, framed under glass, 12" x 24", Rockwell, M, $950.00 C. Courtesy of Mitchell collection.

1919, Marian Davis shown holding a glass, partial pad, framed, matted, under glass example of an early star endorsement, 6" x 10½", EX.......... $3,200.00 C

1920, Garden Girl with bottle, 12" x 32", EX....................$1,950.00 C

1921, Autumn Girl, 12" x 32", EX ....$1,200.00 C

1922, girl at baseball game with a glass, 12" x 32", EX ....$1,600.00 C

1925, girl at party with white fox fur and a glass, 12" x 24". Beware of reproductions. EX...........................$850.00 C

1926, girl in tennis outfit holding a glass, with a bottle sitting by the tennis racquet, 10" x 18", VG...........$850.00 C

1929, flapper girl in green dress, string of beads, glass and bottle, full pad, 12" x 24", EX................................$800.00 C

1929, flapper girl in green dress with string of beads displaying both glass and bottle, full pad, framed under glass, 12" x 24", M...................... $1,025.00 C

1930, woman in swimming attire sitting on rock with canoe in foreground with bottles, partial pad, 12" x 24", EX..$775.00 D

1932, young boy sitting at well with a bucket full of bottles and a dog sitting up at his feet, full pad, framed and under glass, 12" x 24", Rockwell, M, $825.00 C. Courtesy of Mitchell collection.

1933, Village Blacksmith will full pad, framed and under glass, 12" x 24", Frederic Stanley, M, $775.00 C. Courtesy of Mitchell collection.

1934, girl on porch playing music for elderly gentleman with cane, full pad, framed under glass, 12" x 24", Rockwell, M, $750.00 C. Courtesy of Mitchell collection.

1933, the Village Blacksmith with full pad, 12" x 24", Frederic Stanley, EX ....$700.00 C

1934, girl on porch playing music for elderly gentleman with cane, full pad, 12" x 24", Rockwell, EX........$500.00 C

1937, boy walking, fishing pole over his shoulder, holding bottles, 12" x 24", EX ....$550.00 C

1938, girl sitting in front of blinds with a bottle, full pad, framed under glass, Crandall, M .... $695.00 C

1939, girl starting to pour Coca-Cola from bottle into glass, unmarked, full pad, framed under glass, M ..... $550.00 C

1940, woman in red dress with a glass and a bottle, full pad, framed and under glass, VG .... $525.00 C

1941, girl wearing ice skates sitting on log, displaying a bottle, full pad displays two months at same time, VG...$250.00 C

1943, pocket, "Tastes like Home," small, with months shown on front sheet, sailor drinking from a bottle, G...$40.00 C

1942, boy and girl with bottles building snowman, full pad displays two months at once, VG, $325.00 C. Courtesy of Mitchell collection.

1943, military nurse with a bottle, full pad displays two months at once, EX, $475.00 C. Courtesy of Mitchell collection.

1940, woman in red dress with a glass and a bottle, full pad, framed and under glass, VG, $525.00 C. Courtesy of Mitchell collection.

1944, woman holding a bottle, full pad, EX .... $300.00 C

1945, Boy Scout in front of the Scout Oath, Rockwell, M.................$550.00 D

1945, Girl in head scarf with snow falling in the background, full pad, VG........$250.00 C

1946, Boy Scout den chief showing younger Cub Scout how to tie a knot, Rockwell, VG ....$450.00 D

1947, girl holding snow skis with mountains in background, full pad, G... $200.00 C

1949, girl in red cap with a bottle, full pad, M .... $275.00 C

1953, Boy Scout, Cub Scout, and Explorer Scout in front of Liberty Bell, Coca-Cola Bottling Works, Greenwood, Mississippi, Rockwell, VG ....$275.00 C

1953, "Work Better Refreshed," full pad, VG ....$125.00 C

1954, "Me, too!" 1953 Santa cover sheet, full pad, G ....$85.00 C

1954, reference edition with full pad featuring Santa with bottle, VG......$85.00 C

1953, Boy Scout, Cub Scout, and Explorer Scout in front of Liberty Bell, Coca-Cola Bottling Works, Greenwood, Mississippi, matted and framed under glass, Rockwell, EX, $425.00 D. *Courtesy of Mitchell collection.*

1945, girl in head scarf with snow falling in the background, full pad, EX, $325.00 C. *Courtesy of Mitchell collection.*

1958, snow scene of a boy and girl with a bottle, "Sign of Good Taste," full pad, M, $185.00 C. *Courtesy of Mitchell collection.*

1954, sports scene in background with woman in foreground holding a bottle, full calendar pad, M ....$195.00 C

1955, reference edition with Santa holding a bottle, M ....$35.00 C

1957, "The pause that refreshes," girl holding ski poles and a bottle, EX ....$100.00 C

1962, "Enjoy that Refreshing New Feeling," boy holding bottle and offering other hand to dance with a young woman, M .... $80.00 C

1964, "Things go better with Coke," featuring a woman reclining on a couch while a man is offering her a bottle, M ....$85.00 C

1965, "Things go better with Coke," a couple relaxing by a log cabin, each with a bottle, VG .... $85.00 C

1966, man pictured holding serving tray with food and bottles over woman's head, full pad, "Things Go Better with Coke," M ....$90.00 C

1969, "Things go better with Coke," featuring boy whispering into girl's ear while both are seated at a table enjoying a bottle, full pad, M ....$75.00 C

1956, "There's nothing like a Coke," full pad, featuring girl pulling on ice skates, M, $145.00 C. Courtesy of Mitchell collection.

1967, "For the taste you never get tired of," featuring five women with trophy, full pad, M, $65.00 C. Courtesy of Mitchell collection.

1955, woman in hat holding a bottle, full pad, M, $225.00 C. Courtesy of Mitchell collection.

1974, 1927 reproduction, reverse image, full pad, M................................$25.00 D

1975, scenes of America showing backpackers, with full pad, M ....$25.00 C

1978, airborne snow skier, full pad, M..$20.00 D

1979 Olympic torch, full pad, M ....$20.00 C

1980, Sports scenes, full pad, M.....$20.00 D

1981, "Have a Coke and a smile," full pad with scenes of America at top, EX .... $20.00 C

1983, iced-down bottles in front of a bonfire, full pad, M..................$20.00 D

Trays

Change, "Drink a Bottle of Carbonated Coca-Cola," 1903, 5½" dia., G...................................$2,500.00 C

Change, "Drink Coca-Cola Delicious Refreshing," Juanita, 1900s, 4" dia., VG...$500.00 C

Change, "Drink Coca-Cola, Relieves Fatigue," 1907, EX.................$775.00 C

Change, featuring Betty, 1914, EX ....$450.00 C

Change, "Drink Coca-Cola Delicious Refreshing," Juanita, 1900s, 4" dia., EX, $1,000.00 D. Courtesy of Mitchell collection.

Top left: Change, Hamilton King model enjoying a glass, 1913, 4¼" x 6", EX, $625.00 C.

Top right: Change, oval commemorating the St. Louis World's Fair, 1909, 4¼" x 6", EX, $650.00 C.

Change, World War I Girl, 1916, 4⅜" x 6⅛", EX, $375.00 C. Courtesy of Mitchell collection.

Change, featuring the Coca-Cola Girl, 1910, King, VG .... $425.00 C

Change, Hilda Clark, 1901, 6" dia., VG .... $1,250.00 B

Change receiver, ceramic, "The Ideal Brain Tonic" with red lettering, 1890s, 10½" dia., VG .... $4,500.00 C

Change receiver, ceramic, with dark lettering and red outline, "The Ideal Brain Tonic, For Headache and Exhaustion," 1899, F .... $1,200.00 C

Change receiver, glass, "Drink Coca-Cola 5¢," 1907, 7" dia., VG ..... $775.00 C

Change, World War I Girl, 1916, 4⅜" x 6⅛", NM .... $600.00 C

Christmas serving tray, there are many variations of this tray, 1973, VG .... $15.00 D

Commemorative bottlers serving tray from the Lehigh Valley with artwork of plant, 1981, EX .... $15.00 C

General Merchandise, new, painted by Jeanne Mack, inspired by a real location in Georgia where rural neighbors would gather for an ice cold "Coke," 17½" x 12¾", 1997, NM .... $12.00 C

Serving, Autumn Girl, rectangular, 1920s, 10½" x 13¼", VG ...... $775.00 C

Change receiver, glass, "Drink Coca-Cola 5¢," 1907, 7" dia., EX, $1,250.00 C.

Change, Hilda Clark with flowers, 1901, 6" dia., EX, $2,500.00 C.

Change receiver, ceramic, with dark lettering and red line outline, "The Ideal Brain Tonic, For Headache and Exhaustion," 1899, EX, $5,700.00 C.

Change, Hilda Clark at table with stationery holding a glass in a glass holder, 1903, 6" dia., EX, $2,300.00 B.

Serving, Betty, manufactured by Stelad Signs, Passaic, New Jersey, oval, 1914, 12½" x 15¼". Beware of reproductions. G...$200.00 C

Serving, Betty, manufactured by Stelad Signs, Passaic, New Jersey, oval, 1914, 12½" x 15¼", Beware of reproductions. G... $275.00 C

Serving, boy and dog, boy is holding sandwich and a bottle, 1931, 10½" x 13¼", Rockwell, VG..............$775.00 C

Serving, Captain James Cook bicentennial, produced to celebrate landing at Nootka Sound, B.C, "Coca-Cola" on back, 1978, EX........................$35.00 D

Serving, "Coca-Cola" with good litho by Western Coca-Cola Bottling Company of Chicago, Illinois, without the sanction of the Coca-Cola Company, 1908, F ....$975.00 C

Serving, "Coca-Cola" with good litho by Western Coca-Cola Bottling Company of Chicago, Illinois, without the sanction of the Coca-Cola Company, 1908, G...............................$3,200.00 C

Serving, Curb Service for fountain sales, 1928, EX.......................$900.00 B

Serving, "Coca-Cola" with good litho by Western Coca-Cola Bottling Company of Chicago, Illinois, without the sanction of the Coca-Cola Company, 1908, EX, $5,500.00 D. Courtesy of Muddy River Trading Co./Gary Metz.

Serving, rectangular, Coca-Cola Girl holding a glass, 1913, 10½" x 13¼", King, EX, $950.00 C. Beware of reproductions. Courtesy of Mitchell collection.

Serving, Betty, manufactured by Stelad Signs, Passaic, New Jersey, oval, 1914, 12½" x 15¼", EX, $900.00 C. Beware of reproductions. Courtesy of Mitchell collection.

Serving, "Drink Coca-Cola, Delicious and Refreshing," girl on dock, Sailor Girl, 1940, 13¼" x 10½", NM .... $625.00 B

Serving, "Drink Coca-Cola Relieves Fatigue," oval, 1907, 10½" x 13¼", EX ....$2,500.00 B

Serving, "Drink Coca-Cola Relieves Fatigue," oval, 1907, 10½" x 13¼", G... $975.00 C

Serving, "Drive-In," "Drink Coca-Cola" in fishtail logo, "Goes good with food" under logo, "Drive in for Coke" on rim, a hard to find piece, 1959, VG ....$150.00 C

Serving, Elaine, 1916, 8½" x 19", VG...$450.00 D

Serving, featuring a couple receiving curb service, 1927, 13¼" x 10½", P .... $125.00 C

Serving, featuring a couple receiving curb service, 1927, 13¼" x 10½", NM ..$925.00 C

Serving, featuring Betty, rectangular, 1914, 10½" x 13¼", EX .... $825.00 C
Beware of reproductions.

Serving, featuring birdhouse full of flowers, French version, 1950s, 10½" x13¼", VG....................$35.00 D

79

Serving, Coca-Cola Girl, oval, 1913, 12¼" x 14¼", King, EX, $975.00 C.
Courtesy of Mitchell collection.

Serving, featuring a couple receiving curb service, 1927, 13¼" x 10½", G, $750.00 C
Courtesy of Mitchell collection.

Serving, Autumn Girl, this model is featured on the 1922 calendar, rectangular, 1920s, 10½" x 13¼", EX, $1,000.00 C. *Courtesy of Mitchell collection.*

Serving, featuring bottle of Coca-Cola with food, Mexican, 1970, 13¼", M.... $20.00 D

Serving, featuring Elaine, manufactured by Stelad Signs, Passaic Metal Ware Company, Passaic, New Jersey, rectangular, 1916, 8½" x 19". Beware of reproductions. VG .... $475.00 C

Serving, featuring girl on arm of chair in party dress, Hostess, 1936, 10½" x 13¼", VG .... $325.00 C

Serving, featuring girl on beach in chair with a bottle, 1932, 10½" x 13¼", VG .... $475.00 C

Serving, "Drink Coca-Cola Relieves Fatigue," oval, 1907, 10½" x 13¼", EX, $2,500.00 C. *Courtesy of Mitchell collection.*

Serving, featuring movie star Madge Evans, manufactured by American Art Works, Inc, Coshocton, Ohio, 1935, 10½"x 13¼", EX, $425.00 D. Courtesy of Mitchell collection.

Serving, featuring the famous Maureen O'Sullivan and Johnny Weissmuller both holding bottles, 1934, 13¼" x 10½", EX, $975.00 C. Beware of reproductions. Courtesy of Mitchell collection.

Serving, featuring Elaine (modeled by film star Faye Tincher), manufactured by Stelad Signs Passaic Metal Ware Company, Passaic, New Jersey, rectangular, 1916, 8½" x 19", EX, $675.00 C. Beware of reproductions. Courtesy of Mitchell collection.

Serving, featuring girl running on beach with bottles in each hand, 1937, EX ....$375.00 C Beware of reproductions.

Serving, featuring ice skater with bottle on log, 1941, 10½" x 13¼", VG ....$275.00 C

Serving, featuring movie star Madge Evans, manufactured by American Art Works, Inc, Coshocton, Ohio, 1935, 10½"x 13¼", NM ....$550.00 C

Serving, featuring movie star Madge Evans, manufactured by American Art Works, Inc., Coshocton, Ohio, 1935, 10½" x 13¼", F ....$125.00 C

Serving, featuring red-haired woman in yellow scarf with a bottle, 1950s, 10½" x 13¼". Beware of reproductions. VG...$150.00 C

Serving, featuring the Coca-Cola Girl, this was the first rectangular tray used by the Coca-Cola Company by American Art Works, Inc., 1909, 10½" x 13¼", King, EX .... $1,200.00 C Beware of reproductions.

Serving, featuring the famous Maureen O'Sullivan and Johnny Weissmuller both holding bottles, 1934, 13¼" x 10½", NM ....$1,200.00 C Beware of reproductions.

Serving, featuring model Paulene Moore on arm of chair in party dress, Hostess, 1936, 10½" x 13¼", EX, $475.00 C. Courtesy of Mitchell collection.

Serving, featuring girl with ice skates on log and a bottle, 1941, 10½" x 13¼", EX, $375.00 C. Courtesy of Mitchell collection.

Serving, featuring the girl at party, 1921, 10½" x 13¼", G, $500.00 C. Courtesy of Mitchell collection.

Serving, featuring the famous Maureen O'Sullivan and Johnny Weissmuller, 1934, 13¼" x 10½". Beware of reproductions. G ...$400.00 C

Serving, featuring the movie star, Frances Dee, 1933, 10½" x 13¼", G.....$350.00 C

Serving, featuring the Summer Girl, 1922, 10½" x 13¼", VG........$675.00 C

Serving, Flapper Girl, 1923, 10½" x 13¼", G.................................$125.00 C

Serving, Garden Girl, 1920, 13½" x 16½", VG..............................$400.00 C

Serving, girl in afternoon with a bottle, produced by American Art Works Inc., Coshocton, Ohio, 1938, 10½" x 13¼", VG...$200.00 C

Serving, girl in swimsuit holding bottle, promoting bottle sales, 1929, 10½" x 13¼", VG..............................$600.00 C

Serving, girl on a spring board, 1939, 10½" x 13¼", VG.................$250.00 C

Serving, "Hambly's Beverage Limited," featuring World War I girl, 60th anniversary, 1977, EX.............$25.00 D

Serving, Juanita, bottle version, 1906, 10½" x 13½", EX ....$2,500.00 D

Serving, featuring the movie star, Frances Dee, 1933, 10½" x 13¼", EX, $575.00 C. Courtesy of Mitchell collection.

Serving, promoting fountain sales with soda person, 1928, 10½" x 13¼", EX, $675.00 B. Courtesy of Mitchell collection.

Serving, sports couple, 1926, 10½" x 13¼", EX, $850.00 C. Beware of reproductions. Courtesy of Mitchell collection.

Serving, St. Louis Fair, oval, 1909, 13½" x 16½", EX, $2,800.00 C. Courtesy of Mitchell collection.

Serving, Menu Girl, English version, 1950s, 10½" x 13¼", EX.......$125.00 C

Serving, Menu Girl, French version, 1955 – 1960, 10½" x 13¼", EX........$175.00 D

Serving, pansy garden, 1961, 13¼" x 10½", EX ....$30.00 B

Serving, promoting bottle sales, bobbed hair girl drinking from bottle with a straw, 1928, 10½" x 13¼",VG.............$650.00 C

Serving, promoting fountain sales, girl on phone, "meet me at the soda fountain," 1930, 10½" x 13¼",VG............$375.00 C

Serving, rectangular, Coca-Cola Girl holding a glass, 1913, 10½" x 13¼", King, G.................................. $300.00 D Beware of reproductions.

Serving, rectangular, covered bridge with "Coca-Cola" on side, Summer Bridge, 1995, Jim Harrison, EX ....$15.00 D

Serving, red-haired girl with wind in hair on solid background, 1950. Beware of reproductions. EX. ....$200.00 C

Serving, round, featuring University of Indiana basketball, 1976, EX .....$25.00 D

Serving, sports couple, 1926, 10½" x 13¼", NM .... $1,000.00 C Beware of reproductions.

Book, 1942 advertising price list, for advertising, EX, $225.00 B. *Courtesy of Muddy River Trading Co./Gary Metz.*

Book cover, national insignia of planes, 1940s, EX, $35.00 C. *Courtesy of Mitchell collection.*

Book cover for school book, 1940 – 50s, white and red, EX, $10.00 C. *Courtesy of Mitchell collection.*

Paper Goods

Serving, sports couple, 1926, 10½" x 13¼". Beware of reproductions. VG...$725.00 B

Serving, St. Louis Fair, oval, 1909, 13½" x 16½", VG ....$1,800.00 C

Serving, two women at car with bottles, because of metal needed in the war effort this was the last tray produced until after World War II, 1942, NM ....$425.00 C

TV, Duster Girl, 1972, 10¾" x 14¾", EX ....$15.00 D

Victorian Girl, "Drink Coca-Cola, Refreshing, Delicious," woman drinking from a glass, 1897, 9¼" dia., F ....$3,500.00 C

Advertisement from the *Chicago Daily News,* full page, 1908, EX....... $15.00 B

Alphabet Book of Coca-Cola, 1928, VG...$65.00 C

Book, *100 Best Posters,* hardcover, 1941, EX ....$65.00 D

Book, 1942 advertising price list, for advertising, VG......................$195.00 D

Book, 1943 advertising price list, NM ....$265.00 C

Book, 1944 advertising price list, NM ....$300.00 C

Bottlers' advertising price list, 50th Anniversary, 1936, EX, $325.00 C. *Courtesy of Mitchell collection.*

Bottlers' advertising price list, 1935, EX, $235.00 C. *Courtesy of Mitchell collection.*

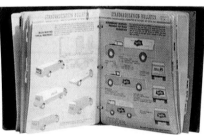

Advertisement from the Chicago Daily News, full page, 1908, EX, $15.00 B. *Courtesy of Muddy River Trading Co./Gary Metz.*

Bulletins book with Coca-Cola bulletins from the '50s and '60s featuring some great information, 1950s, G, $50.00 D. *Courtesy of Muddy River Trading Co./Gary Metz.*

Book, *At Work Handbook Manual,* EX ....$325.00 C

Book, *Illustrated Guide to the Collectibles of Coca-Cola,* Cecil Munsey, 1972, EX....................$90.00 C

Book, *Pause For Living,* bound copy, 1960s, red, EX.........................$15.00 C

Book, sugar ration, 1943, EX ..$30.00 D

Book, *The 5 Star Book,* 1928, EX...$55.00 D

Book, *The Six Bottle Carton for the Home,* illustrated, 1937, EX...$240.00 C

Book, *The Wonderful World of Coca-Cola,* NM ....$85.00 D

Book, *Universal Beverage,* explaining fountain and bottle service, with Elaine, 1915, EX ....$175.00 C

Book, *When You Entertain,* by Ida Bailey Allen, 1932, EX............$20.00 D

Book cover, *America is Strong... because America is Good!* Dwight Eisenhower on front, 1950s, VG...$15.00 C

Booklet, *Coolers for Coca-Cola* with pictures, 1941, EX....................$95.00 C

Coca-Cola News, *3rd edition, dated April 15, 1896, very hard to find, 6" x 8", NM, $135.00 C.*
Courtesy of Muddy River Trading Co./Gary Metz.

Booklet, The Charm of Purity, *1920s, EX, $45.00 C. Courtesy of Mitchell collection.*

Bottlers' advertising price list, 1933, EX, $235.00 C. Courtesy of Mitchell collection.

Booklet, *Easy Hospitality,* 1951, EX..............................$20.00 D

Booklet, *Facts,* 1923, EX.........$65.00 D

Booklet, *Flower Arranging,* 1940, EX...............................$15.00 C

Booklet, *Homes and Flowers,* 1940, EX...............................$12.00 D

Booklet, *Know Your War Planes,* 1940s, EX...............................$65.00 D

Booklet, *Profitable Soda Fountain Operation,* 1953, EX...............$75.00 C

Booklet, *Pure and Healthful,* 1915, G..............................$35.00 B

Booklet, *The Charm of Purity,* 1920s, F...............................$10.00 C

Booklet, *The Charm of Purity,* 1920s, G..............................$35.00 C

Booklet, *The Coca-Cola Bottler,* 1940, EX...............................$40.00 C

Booklet, *The Coca-Cola Bottler,* 1940, P...............................$20.00 C

Booklet, *The Romance of Coca-Cola,* 1916, EX...............................$95.00 C

Paper border display wrap with graphics of Christmas light-up Coke truck, 1996, EX, $50.00 C. Courtesy of Sam and Vivian Merryman.

Paper border with Diet Coke messages, used mainly to cover display bases, full roll, unused, EX, $30.00 C. Courtesy of Sam and Vivian Merryman.

Paper border, corrugated paper for store display use, full unused roll, EX, $30.00 C. Courtesy of Sam and Vivian Merryman.

Booklet, *Transportation by Coca-Cola,* 15 pages with diffferent types of transportation, a school educational tool, 1940s, EX ....$25.00 C

Booklet with woman in front of sundial on front and bottle in hand on back cover, with original envelope, 1923, EX ....$45.00 D

Bottlers' advertising price list, 1933, EX ....$235.00 C

Bottlers' advertising price list, 1935, EX .... $235.00 C

Bottlers' advertising price list, 50th Anniversary, 1936, EX...........$325.00 C

Bottlers' advertising price list, 50th Anniversary, 1936, P..............$125.00 D

Bottlers' advertising price list, January 1932, F ....$90.00 D

Bottlers' magazine, *The Red Barrel*, 1940, EX ....$20.00 D

Bottlers' magazine, *The Red Barrel*, 1940, P ....$12.00 D

Bottling plant guide for educational tours of the plant, 1950s, EX....$15.00 C

Bulletin book for route men, 1950 – 1960s, VG ....$35.00 D

Paper border, corrugated paper for displays with graphics of Santa in chair, full unused roll, EX, $30.00 C. Courtesy of Sam and Vivian Merryman.

Score card for St. Louis National League, Robison Field, 1916, EX, $30.00 C. Courtesy of Mitchell collection.

Magazine cover, front and back, The Housewife, June 1910, framed, The A. D. Poster Co., Publisher, New York, 1910, G, $185.00 C. Courtesy of Mitchell collection.

Bulletins book with Coca-Cola bulletins from the '50s and '60s featuring some great information, 1950s, G......$50.00 D

Cap saver bag, for saving caps to redeem for cash from bottler at Bethlehem, Pa., red & white, 2½" x 5", EX ....$20.00 C

Card hologram, Cal Ripken, McDonald's, and Coke, 1991, NM ......$15.00 D

Carton wrap, "Holiday Hospitality," 1940s, M ....$20.00 D

Catalog sheet, Roy G. Booker Coca-Cola jewelry from "Gifts In Fine Jewelry," 1940, NM ....$75.00 C

Catalog, The All-Star Mechanical Pencil Line, featuring Coca-Cola and other drink lines, 1941, M................$45.00 D

Christmas card with "Seasons Greetings" under silver ornament, 1976, red, M ....$10.00 D

Circus cut-out for kids, still uncut in one piece, 1927, EX ....$350.00 C

Coca-Cola money roll, halves, VG..$6.00 C

Coca-Cola money roll, quarters, M ....$6.00 C

Score pads, "Spotter," "Drink Coca-Cola Delicious and Refreshing," and military nurse in uniform, 1940, EX, $15.00 each C. Courtesy of Mitchell collection.

Newspaper, Paducah Sun-Democrat, June 18, 1939, advertising the opening of a new bottling plant, F, $75.00 C. Courtesy of Mitchell collection.

Handbook, used for sales preparation in retail stores, white lettering on red, 1950s, EX, $25.00 B.

Courtesy of Muddy River Trading Co./Gary Metz.

Comic book, *Refreshment Through The Ages*, 1951, EX ....$30.00 D

Comic trade card featuring woman in bathtub and serving bottles from a serving tray, 1905, beware of reproductions, VG .... $800.00 D

Convention packet, 14th annual Coca-Cola Convention at Philadelphia, 1988, F ....$20.00 C

Coupon, featured 12 pack, 1950s, EX ....$15.00 C

Coupon, for free six pack with return of empty six pack featuring Santa Claus, issued from bottling company in Youngstown, Ohio, white lettering on light green background with Santa in 4-color, 6" x 3", EX ....$10.00 C

Coupon, free bottle of Coke, 1920s, EX ....$20.00 C

Coupon, "Free 6 Bottles of Coca-Cola," pictures six pack with wire handle, 1950s, EX................................$10.00 C

Coupon, good for six pack of Coke when five are accumulated, red and green lettering on light green background, 3½" x 2", EX ....$10.00 C

Paper, St. Louis Cardinals souvenir Score Card, art of woman vendor on back with St. Louis products that make the game more enjoyable, EX, $25.00 C. Courtesy of Mitchell collection.

Wildflower study cards for schools, complete set consists of 20 cards and envelopes, 1920 – 30, VG, $60.00 set D.

Paper, St. Louis Cardinals Official Score Card and Program, with artwork of stadium vendor with Coke bottle, G, $20.00 C. Courtesy of Mitchell collection.

Coupon, "Refresh yourself," free at Roberts & Echols, Glendale, Calif., 1920s, 5" x 2", EX ....$45.00 D

Coupon, 1900, EX..................$400.00 C

Coupon, "This Card Entitles You To One Glass of Coca-Cola," 1903, EX ....$400.00 B

Coupon, "Wholesome Refreshment" with red-headed boy drinking from a bottle with a straw, 1920s, EX..$100.00 D

Coupons, "Refresh Yourself" with bottle in hand, 1920s, EX.............$75.00 C

Display sheet for cartons, "Match the brides for fun and prizes," for 35-cap display, 1967, EX.....................$30.00 C

Driver's route book, EX...........$15.00 D

Famous Doctors Series, set of six heavy folders, complete, of individual figure approximately $35.00 each, 1932, EX ....$250.00 C

Halloween promotional package for dealers, 1954, EX....................$35.00 D

Handbook, "Comprehensive Advertising Price Lists of Items From The 60s," EX ....$150.00 C

Return ticket showing price of returned bottle deposit, G, $15.00 C. Courtesy of Mitchell collection.

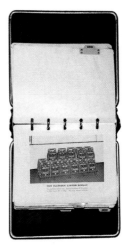

Salesman merchandise book, hardback 5-ring binder, 1942, EX, $400.00 D. Courtesy of Chief Paduke Antiques Mall.

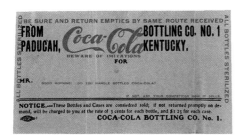

Route coupon from Paducah, Ky., EX, $25.00 C. Courtesy of Mitchell collection.

Handbook, used for sales preparation in retail stores, white lettering on red, 1950s, EX ....$25.00 B

Health record, My Daily Reminder, Compliments of Sanford Coca-Cola Bottling Co., Sanford, N.C. Phone 20, 1930s, G ....$15.00 C

Holder for gas ration book, "Drink Coca-Cola in Bottles," G ....$25.00 D

Information kit, New York World's Fair, "The Coca-Cola Company Pavilion," 1964, NM ....$65.00 D

Kit, merchandising for cooler, 1930, M ....$85.00 D

Letter, Asa G. Chandler, matted and framed, 1889, EX ....$250.00 C

Magazine cover, front and back, *The Housewife,* June 1910, framed, The A. D. Poster Co., Publisher, New York, 1910, G .... $185.00 C

Magazine, vest pocket, complete set of 52, 1928, NM ....$500.00 D

Menu, for soda fountain, matted and framed, 1902, 4⅛," x 6⅛", EX ....$600.00 B

Menu, Hilda Clark, soda menu, matted and framed, hard to find, 1903, 4⅛" x 6⅛", EX ....$650.00 B

*Price list with great colors
and period graphics in book
form, 1941, EX, $325.00 B.
Courtesy of Muddy River Trading
Co./Gary Metz.*

*Slide chart for figuring
profits on sales of Coca-
Cola, G, $20.00 C. Cour-
tesy of Mitchell collection.*

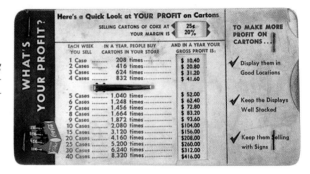

National Geographic Coca-Cola ads, full set, EX ....$315.00 C

Newspaper, *Paducah Sun-Democrat,* June 18, 1939, advertising the opening of a new bottling plant, F .... $75.00 C

Notepad, celluloid, 1902, 2½" x 5", EX ....$600.00 B

Notepad, leather covered, 1905, 2¾" x 4½", EX ....$225.00 D

Notepad, pocket size, white lettering on red, 1943, 4" x 6", EX..............$45.00 D

Notepad with boy and dog, 1931, 10" x 7", Rockwell, EX ....$45.00 D

Opera program presented by Columbus Coca-Cola Bottling Co., 1906, EX ....$125.00 C

Paper advertisment showing a factory whistle and a Coke vending machine, "Inviting workers everywhere to the pause that refreshes with ice cold Coca-Cola," 10" x 13", 1950s, EX ....$10.00 C

Paper book cover featuring the girl drinking from a bottle in front of what appears to be a Westinghouse cooler, opposite is a patriot man, 1940s, EX ....$20.00 C

Sheet music of "My Old Kentucky Home," featuring Juanita on cover with a glass, 1906, EX, $850.00 B.

Slide information booklet, Kit Carson, 1950s, VG, $45.00 C. Courtesy of Mitchell collection.

Paper border, corrugated display paper promoting the "One & Only Taste," EX ....$30.00 C

Paper border, corrugated paper display border with graphics for Super Bowl XXXV, full unused roll, EX ....$35.00 C

Paper border wrap for displays promoting Coca-Cola Classic, 6" tall, NM .... $35.00 C

Paper, St. Louis Cardinals Official Score Card and Program, with artwork of stadium vendor with Coke bottle, G..$20.00 C

Paper, St. Louis Cardinals souvenir Score Card, art of woman vendor on back with St. Louis products that make the game more enjoyable, EX ....$25.00 C

Placemats, "Around The World," set of four, 1950s, EX ....$25.00 C

Price list with great colors and period graphics in book form, 1941, EX .... $325.00 B

Report card holder with 1923 bottle, 1930s, EX................................$85.00 D

Return ticket showing price of returned bottle deposit, G .... $15.00 C

Sheet music for "The Coca-Cola Girl," words and music by Howard E. Way, published by The Coca-Cola Company, Atlanta, Ga., U.S.A, framed, 1927, VG, $325.00 C. Courtesy of Mitchell collection.

Price tag, unused NOS, with Coca-Cola Classic graphic at top, 4" x 8", NM, $5.00 C. Courtesy of Sam and Vivian Merryman.

Route coupon from Paducah, Ky., EX ....$25.00 C

Route coupon from Paducah, Ky., VG...$20.00 C

Salesman merchandise book, hardback 5-ring binder, 1942, EX ....$400.00 D

Score pad for playing cards, six pack in spotlight "easy to serve, good with food," green on white, 4" x 11", EX ....$12.00 D

Service manual and parts catalog for VMC, manufactured Vendolator Mfg. Co. in leatherette book, 1950s, 8" x 9", EX ....$300.00 D

Sheet music for "The Coca-Cola Girl," words and music by Howard E. Way, published by The Coca-Cola Company, Atlanta, Ga., U.S.A, framed, 1927, VG.. $325.00 C

Sheet music of "My Old Kentucky Home," featuring Juanita on cover with a glass, 1906, EX................... $850.00 B

Slide information booklet, Kit Carson, 1950s, VG ....$45.00 C

The Real Coke, The Real Story, hardback, 195 pages, first edition with dustcover, never read, 1986, NM....$18.00 C

Cardboard with rolled paper handle, "Drink Coca-Cola the Pause that Refreshes," 1930, $175.00 C. Courtesy of Mitchell collection.

Cardboard fold out from the Coca-Cola Bottling Co., Bethlehem, Pennsylvania, 1950s, EX, $55.00 C.

"Quality carries on, Drink Coca-Cola" with bottle in hand, 1950, EX, $65.00 C. Courtesy of Mitchell collection.

Rolled paper handle, "Drink Coca-Cola The Pause That Refreshes," Coca-Cola Bottling Co., Martin, Tennessee, EX, $115.00 C. Courtesy of Mitchell collection.

Toonerville cut-out, still uncut and in one piece, 1930, M .... $75.00 C

Writing tablet, Pure As Sunlight, 1930s, EX .... $30.00 D

Writing tablet, wildlife of the United States, 1970s, G .... $10.00 D

Writing tablet, with Silhouette Girl, 1940s, VG .... $18.00 C

Fans

Bamboo with front and back graphics, "Keep Cool, Drink Coca-Cola," Oriental lady drinking a glass of Coca-Cola on opposite side, 1900, F .... $95.00 C

Bamboo with front and back graphics, "Keep Cool, Drink Coca-Cola," Oriental lady drinking a glass of Coca-Cola on opposite side, 1900, VG .... $200.00 C

Cardboard with rolled paper handle, with poem on cover, 1930s, EX .... $195.00 C

Cardboard with wooden handle, "Buy by the carton, 6 for 25¢," Memphis, Tennessee, 1930s, EX .... $185.00 C

Cardboard with wooden handle, "Drink Coca-Cola" with bottle in spotlight, 1930s, EX .... $140.00 C

Canadian blotter with ruler and protractor markings on edges, hard to find piece, 1930s, NM, $275.00 B. Courtesy of Muddy River Trading Co./Gary Metz.

"So Refreshing, Keep on Ice," couple at ice box, 1927, M, $65.00 B.

"Friendliest drink on earth" blotter with bottle in hand and world globe, 1956, 8" x 4", NM, $35.00 C. Courtesy of Sam and Vivian Merryman.

Blotter with the advertising "Restores Energy... Drink Coca-Cola... Strengthens the Nerves," 1926, EX, $125.00 C.

Cardboard with wooden handle from the Coca-Cola Bottling Works of Greenwood, Mississippi, "Enjoy Coca-Cola," 1960s, EX .... $35.00 C

"Drink Coca-Cola" featuring a spotlighted bottle with wooden handle, 1930s, EX................................$85.00 C

Wicker, compliments of Waycross Coca-Cola Bottling Co., 1950s, EX ....$75.00 C

Blotters

50th anniversary of Coca-Cola, "Made In USA, 1936," 7¾" x 3½", 1936, EX ....$25.00 B

"A pure drink of natural flavors," 1929, G..$50.00 C

"Be Prepared," 1950, EX ....$25.00 D

"Be prepared, be refreshed," featuring a Boy Scout offering a Coke from lift top cooler, 7¾" x 3½", 1950, EX ....$200.00 B

Blotter with likeness of young boy on bicycle drinking a bottle of Coke, "The Pause That Refreshes," EX ....$150.00 C

Blotter with the advertising "Restores Energy... Drink Coca-Cola... Strengthens the Nerves," 1926, F......... $35.00 D

Paper blotter with man on bicycle, 7¾" x 3½", EX, $150.00 B. Courtesy of Collectors Auction Services.

"I think it's swell" with graphics of girl lying on her stomach looking at a magazine with an ad of the Sprite Boy, G, $35.00 C. Courtesy of Sam and Vivian Merryman.

Bottle in hand over the earth, 1958, EX ....$25.00 D

Bottle, paper label, "The Most Refreshing Drink in the World," 1904, EX ....$350.00 B

Boy Scout blotter, NOS, with a picture of Boy Scout in front of a wet box cooler drinking a Coca-Cola, 7¾" x 3½", 1942, G...................................$250.00 C

Boy Scouts, "Wholesome Refreshment," 1942, EX ....$25.00 D

"Canadian blotter with ruler and protractor markings on edges, hard to find piece, 1930s, G........................ $75.00 C

Carry A Smile Back To Work Feeling Fit," 1935, M ....$95.00 B

"Coke knows no season," bottle in hand with snow scene in background, 7¾" x 3½", 1947, NM ....$6.00 B

"Cold," dated 1937 in lower left corner, has a Coke bottle in front of a Cold banner, deep, blue background, 7¾" x 3½", 1937, G....................................$18.00 B

"Completely Refreshing," girl on blanket with bottle of Coke, 7¼" x 3¾", 1942, G....................................$15.00 C

"Delicious and Refreshing," fountain service, 1915, EX ....$185.00 B

Paper blotter with girl on beach, 5¾" x 2½", EX, $35.00 B. Courtesy of Collectors Auction Services.

"Refresh Yo'self," white-haired gentleman in hat looking at bottle, 1928, EX, $75.00 D.

Dog and boy with fishing pole, drinking from a bottle, 1930s, EX, $100.00 D.

"Delicious, Refreshing, Invigorating," 1909, red and white, EX.........$120.00 C

Dog and boy with fishing pole, drinking from a bottle, 1930s, G............ $35.00 C

"Drink Coca-Cola," Atlanta, 1904, EX ....$400.00 B

"Drink Coca-Cola," Chicago, 1904, EX ....$120.00 D

"Drink Coca-Cola," with Sprite Boy beside a bottle of Coke, 7¾" x 3½", 1951, VG.................................$13.00 B

Four folks enjoying bottles of Coca Cola in a close setting, Canadian, 1955 EX ....$15.00 C

"Friendliest drink on earth, drink Coca Cola," features a bottle in hand in front of globe, 7¾" x 3½", 1956, EX ......$25.00 B

"Good," Sprite Boy with bottle of Coke in snow bank, with bottle in upper left corner, "Drink Coca-Cola in bottles," 7¾" x 3½", 1953, G.................$10.00 C

"Good with food. Try It," plate of food with two bottles, 1930s, M...... $55.00 D

"The pause that refreshes," 1930, EX, $95.00 B. *Courtesy of Muddy River Trading Co./Gary Metz.*

"How about a Coke," three ladies, each with a bottle of Coke, 7¾" x 3½", 1944, NM ....$20.00 B

"I Think It's Swell," girl, 1942, EX ....$35.00 D

"Over 60 million a day," with large bottle in foreground, 3½" x 7¾", 1960, VG..$12.00 C

Paper blotter with girl on beach, 5¾" x 2½", F .... $10.00 C

Paper blotter with man on bicycle, 7¾" x 3½", G...................................$75.00 B

Paper blotter with Sprite Boy and bottle of Coke, 7¾" x 3½", 1953, EX....... $15.00 B

"Pure and Healthful," with a paper label on each side to promote bottle sales, 1913, EX ....$95.00 D

"Pure as Sunlight", "Drink Coca-Cola, Delicious and Refreshing," "Litho in USA 1931 Courier Journal Lith Louisville," 1931, EX ....$125.00 B

"Refresh Yo'self," white-haired gentleman in hat looking at bottle, 1928, NM .... $135.00 C

"Restores Energy," 1926, red and white, EX ....$130.00 B

99

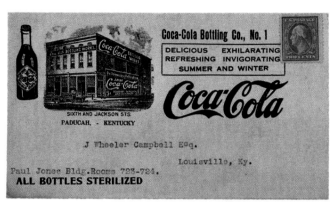

Coca-Cola Bottling Co., No. 1 at Paducah, Ky., with picture of bottling plant at Sixth and Jackson St., 1920s, $65.00 C. Courtesy of Mitchell collection.

International truck, VG, $35.00 C. Courtesy of Mitchell collection.

"So Refreshing, Keep on Ice," couple at ice box, 1927, G ....$15.00 C

"The Drink Everyone Knows," 1939, EX ....$45.00 D

"The most refreshing drink in the world," 1905, EX ....$225.00 C

"The pause that refreshes," 1930, EX .... $95.00 B

Three girls with bottles, disc at right, 1944, NM ....$35.00 C

"Wherever thirst goes," "Drink Coca-Cola," woman in rowboat holding a bottle of Coca-Cola, 5" x 3" (smaller than usual), 1942, M ....$25.00 B

Postcards

Auto delivery truck with an even loaded bed and five men on board, 1913, EX ....$135.00 B

Bottling plant showing interior, 1905, EX ....$135.00 B

Coca-Cola™ girl, 1910, Hamilton King, EX ....$700.00 B

The Coca-Cola Girl, 1910, NM, $775.00 B.
Courtesy of Muddy River Trading Co./Gary Metz.

The Coca-Cola Pavilion at the New York World's Fair, 5½" x 3½", 1964, EX, $10.00 C.

Exterior of a bottling plant showing the truck fleet in front of building, 1906, EX ....$155.00 C

Folding, "Will You Have It – When They Call?," 1913, EX...........$150.00 D

Free six bottles with wire handled carton commemorating 65th Anniversary, 1950s, EX................................$25.00 D

Horse-drawn delivery wagon, 1900, EX ....$135.00 B

Interior of store, 1904, EX ....$100.00 B

Motorized delivery wagon with three men standing beside it, 1915, EX ....$125.00 B

Piccadilly Circus with large Coca-Cola ad, 1950s, VG...........................$10.00 C

Postcard of Poplar Bluff, Missouri, featuring Main Street and a large Coca-Cola sign on top of a building, 1945, EX ....$15.00 C

Postcard featuring picture of DuQuoin, Illinois, bottling plant, NM ......$45.00 D

Magazine ad featuring Lillian Nordica and a coupon at bottom, 1904, NM, $135.00 B.
Courtesy of Muddy River Trading Co./Gary Metz.

Magazine, Christmas ad for "We'll trim the tree. Free," with graphics of a cold bottle of Coke in front of a Christmas scene, 1967, 8½" X 11", VG, $15.00 C. Courtesy of Sam and Vivian Merryman.

Postcard with bottle in hand in center, "Drink ... The Pause That Refreshes," EX ....$15.00 C

Store showing bar with ceramic dispensers and pool table, 1904, EX ....$100.00 D

The Coca-Cola Pavilion at the New York World's Fair, 5½" x 3½", 1964, EX ....$10.00 C.

The Fulton Coca-Cola Bottling Co., 1909, EX ....$150.00 B

Trifold, showing profit for selling Coca-Cola, featuring a teacher at blackboard, 1910s, EX................................$450.00 B

Weldmech truck, 1930, EX......$25.00 D

Ads

"Baseball and coke grew up together," young boy in uniform with a bottle, framed, 1951, 12" x 15", NM ..$15.00 D

Delineator, featuring a city scene, 1921, EX ....$25.00 D

"Drink," glass on ledge, 1917, EX ....$20.00 D

"Face the Day Refreshed," woman at table, "Drink..." button upper left, framed, 1939, 12"x15", EX .....$30.00 D

Christmas together...Have a Coca-Cola

...*welcoming a fighting man home from the wars*

YOUR HOST OF THE AIRWAVES
The Coca-Cola Company presents
EDGAR BERGEN with CHARLIE McCARTHY
CBS 8 p. m. EST every Sunday

And every day...wherever you travel, the familiar red cooler is your
HOST OF THE HIGHWAYS... HOST TO THE WORKER in office
and shop... HOST TO THIRSTY MAIN STREET the country over.

National Geographic *back page, "Christmas together ... Have a Coca-Cola," 1945, 6¾" x 10", G, $8.00 C.*

National Geographic *with Edgar Bergen and Charlie McCarthy, 1950, G, $15.00 C.*

"Get together with refreshment," couple at soda fountain, "Drink..." button upper right, matted and framed, 1941, 12" x 15", NM..........................$20.00 D

Girl with flare glass, 1910s, EX.$25.00 D

Girl with muffler, 1923, NM....$25.00 D

"Has Character," featuring soda person, 1913, VG..................................$15.00 D

Ladies' Home Journal, "Enjoy Thirst," girl, straw and bottle, 1923, NM...$40.00 D

Ladies' Home Journal, girl, background showing golfers, 1922, NM...$40.00 D

Ladies' Home Journal, snow scene and skiers with flare glass in hand, 1922, NM...$25.00 D

Ladies' Home Journal, with ski scene, "Thirst Knows No Season," 1922, EX ....$10.00 C

"Let's Get a Coca-Cola," featuring couple under a fountain service sign, framed, 1939, 12" x 15", EX ....$20.00 D

Magazine ad showing an elaborate soda fountain surrounded by women and children, double page, 9" x 13½", 1905, EX ....$225.00 C

Paper, back cover ad from The Railway Journal, *advertising Coke for 5¢, artwork of engineer and fireman in ICRR locomotive, 8½" x 11", 1929, G, $35.00 C.*

The Housewife *cover, front and back, June 1910, framed, The A.D. Poster Co., Publisher, New York, 1910, G, $185.00 C.*
Courtesy of Mitchell collection.

Magazine, featuring Lillian Nordica and a Coke, matted and framed, 1904, EX ....$110.00 B

Massengale, lady and maid, 1906, EX ....$110.00 B

National Geographic with Edgar Bergen and Charlie McCarthy, 1950, G.. $15.00 C

Newspaper, black and white print of early fountain scene with logo circle arrow, 18" x 21", EX ....$20.00 C

Paper, back cover ad from *The Railway Journal,* advertising Coke for 5¢, artwork of engineer and fireman in ICRR locomotive, 8½" x 11", 1929, G.. $35.00 C

People waiting behind counter, matted and framed, 1905, 14" x 10", EX ....$120.00 B

"Refreshment through the years," "Drink..." button lower right, 1951, 12" x 15", EX ....$15.00 D

Saturday Evening Post, water skier, EX ....$15.00 D

Biedenharn Candy Co., Vicksburg, Miss., embossed block print, Hutchinson Bottle, 1894 – 1902, aqua, EX, $600.00 D.

Biedenharn Candy Co., Vicksburg, Miss., with script "Coca-Cola" on base edge, all embossed, 1905, aqua, EX, $135.00 D.

"Through 65 Years," one side 1886 fountain service, other side 1951 fountain service, framed, 1951, 12" x 15", NM ....$65.00 C

Woman's World, 1920, EX ....$45.00 D

Bottles & Cans

75th Anniversary, Paducah Coca-Cola Bottling Company, Inc., 1978, 10 oz., clear, EX ....$25.00 D

75th Anniversary, Thomas Bottling Company, 1974, amber, EX .....$75.00 C

America's Cup, 1987, NM ....$45.00 D

Analyst-Portfolio Managers Meeting, limited edition of 408 bottles produced, 1996, M ....$250.00 D

Annie Oakley Days LE commemorative, 1985, NM ....$80.00 D

Atlanta Olympics, 1996, NM.....$8.00 D

Baskin Robbins LR commemorative bottle, NM ....$150.00 D

Can with the diamond pattern, unopened, red, 12 oz., EX, $75.00 B.
Courtesy of Collectors Auction Services.

Canadian with white lettering on clear glass with screw on top, 40 oz., clear, EX, $35.00 C.

Biedenharn Candy Co., Vicksburg, Miss., embossed block print, Hutchinson Bottle, 1894 – 1902, aqua, EX ....$600.00 D

Biedenharn Candy Co., Vicksburg, Miss., embossed lettering, block print on crown top bottle, 1900s, aqua, EX ....$325.00 D

Biedenharn Candy Co., Vicksburg, Miss., with script "Coca-Cola" on base edge, all embossed, 1905, aqua, EX ....$135.00 D

Biedenharn Candy Company with applied paper label and "Coca-Cola" in script on bottle shoulder, 1905, aqua, EX ....$400.00 D

Bill Elliot #94, limited edition, commemorative bottle, full, 6½ oz., NM ....$8.00 C

Block print "Coca-Cola" in center of bottle body, fluted above and below name, EX ....$25.00 D

Bobby Labonte #18 limited edition, commemorative bottle, 6½ oz., NM ....$8.00 C

Block print embossed on shoulder, bottle is unusual due to size and color, 32 oz., green, EX, $75.00 D.

Can, waxed paper, a prototype can that was never put into production, dynamic wave contour, red, 12 oz., EX, $135.00 B. Courtesy of Collectors Auction Services.

Bottles, Martha's Vineyard, limited edition commemorative bottle, full, 8 oz., 1997, NM ....$9.00 C

Brickyard 400 Nascar Inaugural at Indianapolis, NM..........................$55.00 D

California State Fair LE commemorative bottle, 1995, NM...............$10.00 D

Can, alternating red and white diamonds, red "Coca-Cola" next to white "Coke" on center diamond, 1960s, VG..$50.00 C

Can, experimental fashioned to feel like bottle, red and white Coca-Cola logo, not put into production, 1990s, 12 oz., NM ....$4.50 C

Can from St. Martin advertising "Carnival 1997" with dynamic wave trademark, 11¼ oz., 1997, EX ....$5.00 C

Can with the diamond pattern, unopened, red, 12 oz., EX........$75.00 B

Carbonation tester used before the introduction of pre-mix, extremely hard to locate since normally only the bottlers had these items, EX................$650.00 B

Biedenharn Candy Co., Vicksburg, Miss., embossed lettering, block print on crown top bottle, 1900s, aqua, EX, $325.00 D.

Block print embossed on base with fluted sides, 7 oz., clear, EX, $40.00 D.

Ceramic syrup jug with paper label, tall, two-color stoneware, hardest to find, 1900s, 10" tall, VG.............$2,600.00 B Beware of reproductions.

Charleston, South Carolina, straight sided bottle with Coca-Cola inscribed on the base, 6½ oz., 1920s, EX ....$35.00 C

Chattanooga 100 years, LE gold cap bottle, issued to commemorate the world's first bottler and 100 years of service, full, 8 oz., 1999, NM.....$8.00 C

Coca-Cola Enterprises LE bottle issued to employees to commemorate their 10th anniversary, full, 8 oz., 1996, NM ....$20.00 B

Coca-Cola safe truck driving rodeo limited edition commemorative, M...$160.00 D

Commemorative Hutchinson style, Coca-Cola 1894 – 1979, 1979, 7¼", M...$130.00 D

Commemorative reproduction of 1927 bottle used on luxury liners, green glass with green and red label, foil covered neck and top, 1994, M ....$75.00 D

Gold, 50th Anniversary 1899 –
1949, Everett Pidgeon in bottle
cradle, 1949, EX, $200.00 C. Cour-
tesy of Mitchell collection.

Carbonation tester used before the introduction of pre-mix, extremely hard to locate since normally only the bottlers had these items, EX, $650.00 B.

Contour can issued to feel similar to the Coke bottle that is so well known, limited issue on a trial basis, didn't work, 12 oz., 1970s, EX .... $6.00 C

Convention, Chicago, Illinois, 1964, EX ....$55.00 C

Convention, Chicago, Illinois, 1972, EX ....$45.00 C

Convention, Chicago, Illinois, 1984, EX ....$40.00 C

Convention, Chicago, Illinois, 1990, EX ....$25.00 C

Convention, Cleveland, Ohio, 1956, EX ....$95.00 C

Convention, Dallas, Texas, 1975, EX ....$55.00 D

Convention, Dallas, Texas, 1986, EX ....$35.00 C

Convention, Detroit, Michigan, 1968, EX ....$50.00 D

Convention, Houston, Texas, 1971, EX ....$45.00 C

Convention, Houston, Texas, 1983, EX ....$40.00 C

Contour can issued to feel similar to the Coke bottle that is so well known, limited issue on a trial basis, didn't work, 12 oz., 1970s, $10.00 C.

Ceramic syrup jug with paper label, tall, two-color stoneware, hardest to find, 1900s, 10" tall, VG, $2,600.00 B. Beware of reproductions. Courtesy of Muddy River Trading Co./Gary Metz.

Convention, Las Vegas, Nevada, 1989, EX ....$30.00 C

Convention, Miami, Florida, 1955, EX ....$95.00 C

Convention, Miami, Florida, 1965, EX ....$50.00 D

Convention, Miami, Florida, 1973, EX ....$45.00 C

Convention, Philadelphia, Pennsylvania, 1954, EX ....$95.00 C

Convention, Philadelphia, Pennsylvania, 1970, EX ....$95.00 C

Convention, San Francisco, California, 1950, EX ....$700.00 C

Convention, San Francisco, California, 1961, EX ....$700.00 C

Convention, St. Louis, Missouri, 1959, EX ....$85.00 C

Dale Earnhardt Sr. and Jr., with artwork of both drivers' cars on front and back, "Coca-Cola 500 Montegi, Japan November 21, 1998," 8 oz., 1998, NM ....$4.00 C

Gold, 100th Anniversary, 1986, EX, $55.00 C. Courtesy of Mitchell collection.

Glass display 1923 Christmas bottle with display cap, 1930s, 20" tall, F, $250.00 B. Courtesy of Muddy River Trading Co./Gary Metz.

Denver Broncos LE commemorative bottle, issued to commemorate the back-to-back Super Bowl Championships, 8 oz., 1999, NM ....$5.00 C

Denver Broncos LE Commemorative issued to celebrate the win of Super Bowl XXXII, 8 oz., 1998, NM ..$5.00 C

Detroit Red Wings, NM ....$5.00 D

Display bottle with cap and patent date, 1923, 20" tall, EX...................$450.00 C

Double diamond with script "Coca-Cola" inside diamond from Toledo, Ohio, 1900 – 1910, 6 oz., amber, EX ....$155.00 C

Easter Seals commemorative, M...$30.00 D

Elvis Presley's Graceland limited edition commemorative bottle, full, 8 oz., 1998, NM ....$6.00 C

Elvis "Still Rockin," limited edition, commemorative, neck has "Graceland 15th Anniversary," body has a guitar and reads "Elvis Still Rockin," 8 oz., 1997, NM. ....$10.00 C

Emergency Coca-Cola bottle, bottle in oak box with plexiglas front and a small mallet to break glass in case of emergency, 8 oz., NM ....$30.00 B

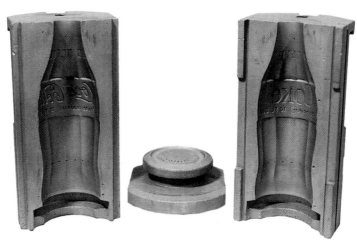

Mold made of solid iron, for 10 oz. no return bottle, very heavy, EX, $425.00 D.

England Royal Wedding, featuring Union Jack flag with screw-on cap, 7-29-81, 8 oz., M.........................$75.00 D

Florida Marlins, 1994, NM........$8.00 D

Georgia State Champions, East Marietta 1983 All Stars World Champions, 10 oz., 1983, NM ....$7.00 B

Georgia Tech National Football Champions LE, issued to commemorate the Yellow Jackets #1 victory, season schedule and scores, 10 oz., 1990, EX ....$6.00 C

Girlstown 50th Anniversary and Cal Farley's Boy's Ranch 60th Anniversary limited edition commemorative bottle, full, 8 oz., 1999, NM.................$8.00 C

Glass display 1923 Christmas bottle with display cap, 1930s, 20" tall, F .... $250.00 B

Glass jug with hoops at neck and embossed lettering, "Coca-Cola" in script, fairly rare, 1900s, one gallon, clear, EX............................$1,200.00 C

Glass jug with round paper label, 1910s, one gallon, clear, EX..............$300.00 B

Limited edition 4-H bottle, "Kentucky Leadership Center, Developing Leaders for Kentucky's Youth," 10 oz., 1986, EX, $45.00 C.

National Convention, 75th Anniversary Hutchinson style bottle, fairly scarce, 1961, light aqua, EX, $250.00 D.

Gold, 50th Anniversary 1899 – 1949, Everett Pidgeon in bottle cradle, 1949, G ....$100.00 C

Gold, 100th Anniversary, 1986, F ....$10.00 C

Gold bottle of Bellingrath Gardens & Homes, Mobile, Alabama, limited edition, NM ....$40.00 D

Gold dipped, "Bottled from the one millionth gallon December 22, 1959, by the Coca-Cola Bottling Co., Memphis, Tennessee," 1959, NM.......................$45.00

Hardee's LE commemorative celebrating opening of the 3000th restaurant, 1988, NM ....$60.00 D

Hardee's 35th anniversary LE commemorative, NM ....$85.00 D

Hawaii Mickey Mouse Toontown limited edition, 1994, NM ....$20.00 D

Head Yai, Thailand, new bottling plant, rare, 1993, 10 oz., NM...........$100.00 D

House for Coca-Cola, August 3, 1977, 10 oz., 1977, NM ....$15.00 C

Premix, 1920s, green, EX, $65.00 C. Courtesy of Mitchell collection.

"Property of Coca-Cola Bottling Co., La Grange, Texas," in block print on body with embossed ribbon on shoulder, 6 oz., aqua, EX, $50.00 C. Courtesy of Mitchell collection.

Hutchinson style, "Birmingham Coca-Cola Bottling Co.," "DOC 13" on back, 1894, 7", NM......................$1,000.00 B

Independent Grocers Alliance, 70th anniversary commemorative, only 960 produced, 1996, M ....$115.00 C

Jacksonville Jaguars LE commemorative No. 1, M............................$5.00 D

Jacksonville Jaguars LE commemorative No. 2, M............................$5.00 D

Jacksonville Jaguars LE commemorative No. 3, M............................$5.00 D

Jeff Gordon #24, LE commemorative bottle, neck reads 1995 Winston Cup Champion (second of two Jeff Gordon Coke bottles), body of bottle reads Jeff Gordon 7 Wins – 8 Poles – 2610 Laps Led, 8 oz., 1995, NM ....$20.00 C

KC Chiefs 35th AFL-NFL 35th Anniversary LE bottle, 8 oz., 1993, NM ....$8.00 C

Kyle Petty #44 LE commemorative bottle, has likeness of Petty over checkered flag on bottle center, 8 oz., NM .$10.00 C

Lamp with embossed "Coca-Cola" base, 1970s, 20", EX ....$6,000.00 C

Oklahoma Anniversary, regular capped, gold dipped with white lettering, dated 1903 – 1967 on reverse, only 1,000 made make this a fairly scarce item, 1967, 6½ oz., gold, EX, $150.00 C.

Script "Coca-Cola" at bottom, from any location, 1910s, 6 oz., amber, EX, $75.00 C.

Leaded glass display bottle, 1920s, 36" tall, EX .... $9,500.00 C

Limited edition 4-H bottle, "Kentucky Leadership Center, Developing Leaders for Kentucky's Youth," 10 oz., 1986, F .... $10.00 D

Long John Silver's LE commemorative, 8 oz., NM ....$95.00 C

Los Angeles Olympics set in boxes with tags, 1984, EX......................$100.00 D

McDonald's Hawaii I, M ....$60.00 D

Mexican Christmas commemorative, 1993, M...................................$26.00 D

Mexico, Christmas with Santa and girl, NM...$8.00 D

Mickey Mouse Hawaii Toontown limited edition commemorative, given away with $200 grocery purchase in Hawaii between May and July 1994, M..$15.00 C

Mold made of solid iron, for 10 oz. no return bottle, very heavy, G..$200.00 D

NASCAR LE commemorative bottle with a checkered flag and "Official Soft Drink of NASCAR," 8 oz., 1998, NM ....$8.00 C

Rubber display bottle, 43" tall, 1940s, G, $850.00 B. Courtesy of Muddy River Trading Co./Gary Metz.

"Root" commemorative bottle is a reissue of the original bottle design of 1915. The original bottle bottoms were plain, the reissue is marked; only 5,000 of the reissues were made, 1965, EX, $425.00 C. Courtesy of Mitchell collection.

Nashville, Tenn., LE commemorative bottle with Coca-Cola in Hebrew and the Star of David on one side and English on the other side, full, 6½ oz., EX ....$12.00 C

National Champions Georgia Bulldogs, LE commemorative bottle, with season schedule and final scores, full, 10 oz., 1980, EX ....$10.00 C

National Convention, 75th Anniversary Hutchinson style bottle, fairly scarce, 1961, light aqua, F ....$55.00 D

New Coke, Houston Coca-Cola Bottling Company, with the introduction of New Coke, one side shows the 100 years of success, the other celebrates the introduction of the new product, 10 oz., 1985, NM ....$15.00 C

North Dakota Centennial limited edition commemorative bottle, empty, 10 oz., EX ....$10.00 C

Oklahoma Anniversary, regular capped, gold dipped with white lettering, dated 1903 – 1967 on reverse, only 1,000 made make this a fairly scarce item, 1967, 6½ oz., gold, G.............. $75.00 C

Script "Coca-Cola" midway, from any location, 1910s, 6 oz., amber, EX, $65.00 C.

Script "Coca-Cola" on shoulder, from any location, 1910s, 6 oz., amber, EX, $70.00 C.

Orange T, LE issued to celebrate the '98 winning season of Tennessee, full, 8 oz., 1997, NM ....$10.00 C

Orlando World Cup, NM ....$10.00 D

Pete Rose, NM ....$100.00 C

Pharmor, NM ....$275.00 D

Piggly Wiggly 50th Anniversary LE bottle, hard to find, distribution based on Piggly Wiggly employees and best 100 customers, 8 oz., 1999, NM ....$10.00 C

Premix, 1920s, green, G.......... $45.00 C

"Property of Coca-Cola Bottling Co., La Grange, Texas," in block print on body with embossed ribbon on shoulder, 6 oz., aqua, P ....$8.00 C

"Root" commemorative bottle is a reissue of the original bottle design of 1915. The original bottle bottoms were plain, the reissue is marked; only 5,000 of the reissues were made, 1965, G..........$275.00 D

Root Commemorative in box with gold clasp, 1965, aqua, EX ....$450.00 D

Rubber display bottle, 43" tall, 1940s, G... $850.00 B

Syrup, with original metal cap, 1920s, EX, $675.00 C. Courtesy of Mitchell collection.

White lettering on clear glass with tight fitting plastic top, used as a display piece, 1960s, 20" tall, clear, EX, $225.00 C.

Sam Houston Bicentennial Birthday limited edition commemorative bottle, with likeness of Sam Houston beside a star, banner that reads "1793 – Bicentennial Birthday Celebration – 1993," 8 oz., 1993, NM ....$5.00 C

San Diego, California, LE commemorative bottle issued to celebrate the 75th anniversary of the bottler, unopened, full and in the original box, 10 oz., 1985, NM ....$20.00 C

Santa Claus Christmas bottle carrier sleeve, Santa Claus & Christmas Greetings, 1930s, M.....................$1,900.00 B

Script "Coca-Cola" at bottom, from any location, 1910s, 6 oz., amber, EX .... $75.00 C

Script "Coca-Cola" midway, from any location, 1910s, 6 oz., amber, EX .... $65.00 C

Script "Coca-Cola" on base edge, "Bottling WKS 2nd Registered" in block print at bottom of base, 1910s, 6½ oz., amber, EX............................. $110.00 C

Super Bowl XXIX, Joe Robbie Stadium, Jan. 25, 1995, LE commemorative bottle, 8 oz., 1995, NM ....$4.00 C

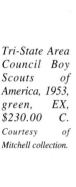

Tri-State Area Council Boy Scouts of America, 1953, green, EX, $230.00 C.
Courtesy of Mitchell collection.

Script "Coca-Cola" on base edge, "Bottling WKS 2nd Registered" in block print at bottom of base, 1910s, 6½ oz., amber, EX, $110.00 C.

Syrup, with original metal cap, 1920s, EX ....$675.00 C

Tri-State Area Council Boy Scouts of America, 1953, green, EX......$230.00 C

Tyber Island Centennial LE commemorative, 10 oz., M ....$8.00 C

University of Georgia, 4-H LE, commemorating Rock Eagle, world's largest 4-H center with 30 years of service, 1954 – 1984, full, 10 oz., 1984, EX ....$10.00 C

Varsity 70th Anniversary, LE commemorative bottle, 1928 – 1998, 8 oz., 1998, NM ....$55.00 B

Wal-Mart 25th Anniversary, LE commemorative bottle, 10 oz., 1987, NM ....$15.00 C

White Castle 75th anniversary LE commemorative bottle, NM ....$85.00 C

White lettering on clear glass with tight fitting plastic top, used as a display piece, 1960s, 20" tall, clear, EX .... $75.00 D

World Cup USA Soccer, LE bottle sold in a tube bank, full, 8 oz., 1994, NM ....$10.00 B

World of Coca-Cola 5th anniversary LE commemorative, 8 oz., M ....$6.00 D

Anniversary glass given to John W. Boucher, 1936, NM, $375.00 B. Courtesy of Muddy River Trading Co./Gary Metz.

50th Anniversary, gold-dipped with plastic stand, 1950s, EX, $250.00 B. Courtesy of Muddy River Trading Co./Gary Metz.

World Series, Dizzy Dean Graduate League Aug. 4-8, Rossville, Georgia, LE commemorative issued by the Chattanooga, Tennessee, Coca-Cola Bottling Co., 10 oz., 1982, NM..............$15.00 C

York Rite Masonry, NM...........$25.00 D

Glasses

50th Anniversary, gold-dipped with plastic stand, 1950s, EX ....$250.00 B

Anniversary glass given to John W. Boucher, 1936, NM...............$375.00 B

Arrow flare, small, acid etched with syrup line at bottom, "Drink Coca-Cola 5¢," 1912 – 1913, EX............ $875.00 B

Bell, "Drink Coca-Cola," 1940 – 1960s, EX................................$15.00 C

Bell, "Enjoy Coca-Cola," 1970s, VG ....$8.00 C

Flare with syrup line, 1900s, EX ....$450.00 C

Information paper showing all the strong points of the glass, VG...$15.00 C

Sugar bowl complete with lid, "Drink Coca-Cola," 1930, M, $375.00 C; Creamer, "Drink Coca-Cola," 1930s, VG, $325.00 C. Courtesy of Mitchell collection.

Pewter, "Coca-Cola," with original leather pouch, 1930s, EX ....$750.00 B

China

Dish, round, world, 1967, 7" EX ..$125.00 C

Dish, square, "Coca-Cola" world, 1960s, 11½", EX ....$135.00 C

Display bottle with original tin lid, 1923 bottle, 20", EX ....$260.00 D

Pitcher, red lettered "Coca-Cola" on glass, M ....$135.00 C

Plate, Swedish, 1969, 8¼" x 6¼", EX ....$100.00 C

Sandwich plate, "Drink Coca-Cola Refresh yourself," 1930s, 8¼", NM ...., $1,200.00 B

Art Plates

Western Coca-Cola™ Bottling Co., featuring brunette with red hair scarf, holding a pink rose, 1908 – 1912, EX ....$425.00 C

Western Coca-Cola™ Bottling Co., featuring dark-haired woman with low drape across shoulders, 1908, 10" dia., EX ....$400.00 C

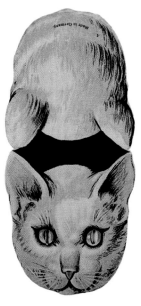 

Pocket mirror, folding cardboard cat's head, "Drink Coca-Cola in bottles" on inside cover, 1920, EX, $825.00 C. Courtesy of Mitchell collection.

Western Coca-Cola™ Bottling Co., featuring long-haired woman body forward with head and eyes to the right wearing a white drape covering off the shoulders, 1908 – 1912, EX.......... $450.00 C

Western Coca-Cola™ Bottling Co., featuring woman with auburn colored hair with a red adornment on the right side of her head, 1908, 10", EX.....$375.00 C

Western Coca-Cola™ Bottling Co., if any art plate is in its original shadow box frame value can be doubled, 1908 – 1912, EX .... $900.00 C

Western Coca-Cola™ Bottling Co., profile of dark-haired woman with red head piece and yellow blouse, 1908 – 1912, 10", EX................................. $400.00 C

Mirrors

Celluloid and metal, "Drink Coca-Cola," Elaine, 1916, 1¾" x 2¾", NM ....$625.00 C

Celluloid and metal, "Drink Coca-Cola," Golden Girl, 1920, 1¾" x 2¾". Beware of reproductions. EX..............$700.00 C

Celluloid and metal, girl on beach beside parasol, much sought after piece, 1922, 1¾" x 2¾", EX ....$1,750.00 D

Metal, "Drink Coca-Cola in Bottles, Quality Refreshment," features button at top, 1950s, EX, $195.00 C. *Courtesy of Mitchell collection.*

Metal, French Canadian bottlers' thermometer, logo at top left with scale on left next to bottle, "Leo Aboussafy," 6" x 16", NM, $350.00 B. *Courtesy of Muddy River Trading Co./Gary Metz.*

Celluloid and metal, Juanita, 1906, 1¾" x 2¾". Beware of reproductions. EX ....$625.00 C

Celluloid and metal, the Coca-Cola Girl, 1910, 1¾" x 2¾", Hamilton King, NM ....$575.00 C

Commemorative wall mirror featuring Hilda Clark, produced for the 75th anniversary of the Chicago Coca-Cola Bottling Co., 1976, 28½" x 41", NM ....$425.00 C

"Drink Coca-Cola in Bottles," Coca-Cola Bottling Co, Madisonville, Kentucky, 1920 – 1930s, 8" x 17½", VG ....$550.00 C

Glass, Silhouette Girl, with thermometer, 1939, 10" x 14¼", VG ....$850.00 B

In frame under glass "Drink Coca-Cola in Bottles Delicious Refreshing," 1930s, 8" x 12", EX...........................$175.00 D

Pemberton and Chandler with ceramic dispenser in center, 1977, M ....$50.00 D

Pocket mirror, "Wherever you go you will find Coca-Cola at all fountains 5¢," 1900s, G .... $900.00 C

123

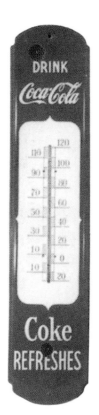

Thermometer, rare prototype, 15" square, EX, $650.00 B. Courtesy of Muddy River Trading Co./Gary Metz.

Porcelain advertising thermometer with the message "Drink Coca-Cola ... Coke refreshes," scale in center, 1940s, 8" x 36", F, $750.00 B. Courtesy of Muddy River Trading Co./Gary Metz.

Thermometers

Cardboard pre-mix counter unit thermometer with mercury scale on left then comparison chart of thermometer reading to regulator setting, 1960s, VG.....................................$65.00 C

Desk, free-standing in leather case with a round dial, hard to find, 1930s, 3¼" x 3¼", EX ....$1,500.00 C

Dial, with gold bottle outline on red center button, black numbers on face, 1908, 12" dia., NM.................$375.00 C

"Drink Coca-Cola, Delicious and Refreshing," Silhouette Girl, 1930s, 6½" x 16", EX........................$475.00 C

Masonite, "Thirst knows no season," 1940s, 6¾"x 17", EX ....$455.00 C

Metal and plastic, Pam, "Drink Coca-Cola Be Really Refreshed," with fishtail, 1960s, 12" dia., NM........$500.00 C

Metal "cigar" thermometer, red & white, 1950s, 30" tall, VG......$175.00 C

Metal, die cut bottle thermometer, 1956, 5" x 17", NM......................... $160.00 B

Bent wood with rounded corners and flat wood handle, 1940s, VG, $135.00 C. Courtesy of Mitchell collection.

Aluminum six pack king size carrier with wire handle, red lettered "Drink Coca-Cola" and "King Size," 1950, EX, $115.00 C. Courtesy of Mitchell collection.

Metal, embossed Spanish bottle thermometer, 1950s, 6" x 18", EX .... $150.00 B

Oval, Christmas bottle, 1938, 6¾" x 16", EX .... $300.00 C

Plastic, "Enjoy Coca-Cola" vertical scale type thermometer, 7" x 18", G .... $30.00 C

Plastic, "Enjoy Tab," vertical scale thermometer with message box at bottom, EX .... $45.00 C

Tin, "Drink Coca-Cola in Bottles," Phone 612, Dyersburg, Tennessee, with reminder notations for oil, grease, and battery, 1940s, VG .... $50.00 C

Wooden, "Coca-Cola 5¢," good graphics, red on white, 1905, 5" x 21", G. $400.00 B

Wooden, "Drink Coca-Cola in Bottles 5¢ Everywhere," V.O. Colson Co., Paris, Illinois, 1910s, VG ...... $675.00 C

Carriers

Cardboard carton display, "Take enough home today," 1950s, 14" x 20" x 8", EX .... $235.00 C

Cardboard, six pack "Money back bottles return for deposit," dynamic wave logo, red and white, NOS, 1970s, EX .... $15.00 D

125

Metal and wire case carrier with wire handles, red on white, 1950 – 1960s, G $65.00 C. Courtesy of Muddy River Trading Co./Gary Metz.

Aluminum six pack with wire handle, separated bottle compartments, "Delicious Refreshing Coca-Cola" in white on red center panel, 1950s, EX, $65.00 C. Courtesy of Mitchell collection.

Cardboard six pack, red background, 1930s, EX..............................$120.00 C

Cardboard, 12 regular size bottles, yellow on red, 1950s, EX ....$20.00 D

Cardboard, 24 bottle case, 1950s, EX ....$50.00 D

Cardboard, white lettering on red, "Chill ... Serve ..." banner at top by cut out carry handle, 12 bottles, NOS, 1950s, EX..................................$25.00 C

Cardboard with metal handles, "Drink Coca-Cola" on front, "Have a Coke," "Picnic Cooler" on sides, red with white lettering, 1956, NM................$155.00 D

Cardboard with wire handle, white lettering on red, six bottle, NOS, 1950s, NM..$50.00 D

Metal and wire Canadian carrier and vendor for 18 bottles "Drink Coca-Cola Iced" on side panels, 1930s, 18 bottle, G.....$285.00 C

Metal carton display rack, 25¢ per six pack, 55" tall, 1930s, VG ...... $500.00 B

Metal for car window, 1940s, white and red, EX ....$75.00 D

Metal grocery cart two bottle holder with sign on front "Enjoy Coca-Cola While You Shop, Place Bottles Here," 1950s, EX.................................$65.00 C

Cardboard six pack, red background, 1930s, EX, $120.00 C. Courtesy of Mitchell collection.

Cardboard six pack, "Serve Ice Cold," 1930s, EX, $135.00 C. Courtesy of Mitchell collection.

Plastic miniature six pack carrying case, red lettering on white, 1970s, EX .$10.00 D

Plastic six pack carrier, King Size, white lettering, 1950s, red, EX ....$15.00 D

Salesman's sample for bulk case storage, 1960s, 6" x 12" x 13", EX...$4,500.00 C

Six pack cardboard, French, 1934, G................................$85.00 C

Six pack carton wrapper, July 4th, 1930s, red, white, and blue, EX ....$350.00 C

Tin, carton rack with great rare sign at top, hard to find, 1930s, 5' tall, NM .... $825.00 B

Vinyl, 12 bottle, white lettering on red, 1950s, EX.................................$35.00 D

Wire and metal bottle rack built in three tiers with "Drink Coca-Cola" button at top, unusual piece, 1940s – 50s, F......$290.00 B

Wire and metal stadium carrier with "Drink Coca-Cola Iced" signs on each side, will hold 24 bottles or cups of the delicious Coca-Cola, F .... $450.00 B

Wire carrier, case size with embossed aluminum, "Drink Coca-Cola," 1940s, 24 bottle, EX .... $45.00 D

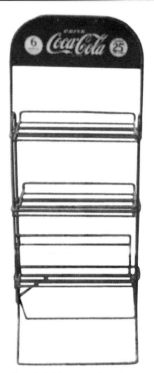

Metal grocery cart two bottle holder with sign on front "Enjoy Coca-Cola While You Shop, Place Bottles Here," 1950s, EX, $65.00 C. Courtesy of Mitchell collection.

Metal rack with folding metal shelves, 47" tall, 1940 – 1950s, EX, $225.00 B. Courtesy of Muddy River Trading Co./Gary Metz.

Wire case rack with "Take some Coca-Cola home today" sign at top of rack, metal wheels on bottom, EX......$285.00 C

Wooden, "Drink Coca-Cola in Bottles," with cut out carrying handle, wings at end, 1940s, yellow, G...............$95.00 C

Wooden six pack carrier with bottle separators, "Pause ... Go refreshed," white on red, 1930s, EX..................$450.00 B

Wooden six pack, "Six bottles for 25¢ plus deposit," 1940s, red, EX....$150.00 C

Wooden six pack, with hand in bottle and wings logo on both ends, G......$125.00 C

Wooden with dovetail corner joints, "Refresh yourself Drink Coca-Cola in Bottles," black lettering, 1920s, VG...$275.00 C

Vending Machines

Cavalier C-27, chest type machine that looks more like an upright, dispenses 27 bottles, uncommon, can be difficult to locate but most collectors could find one with a few contacts, 1940 – 1950s, 18" x 41" x 22", red, VG.....$1,100.00 C

Cavalier C-27 vending machine, 18" x 22" x 41", 1940 – 1950s, EX..$1,400.00 B

Cavalier cooler, holds 2 cases, and works on the honor system since it wasn't equipped with a vending mechanism, red, silver, and white, 18⅛" x 18½" x 40¾", 1940 – 1950s, EX, $1,595.00 D. *Courtesy of Riverside Antique Mall.*

Cavalier wet box, with embossing on inside of lid and on all sides, open to the rack, white on red, EX, $695.00 D. *Courtesy of Affordable Antiques/Oliver Johnson.*

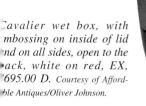

Cavalier C-27 vending machine, 18" x 22" x 41", 1940 – 1950s, EX, $1,400.00 B. *Courtesy of Muddy River Trading Co./Gary Metz.*

Cavalier C-51, upright that will dispense 51 bottles with a precooling shelf under the dispensing unit, 1950s, red, EX ....$550.00 C

Cavalier CS-72, 24¾" x 21⅞", 1950s, EX ....$1,850.00 C

Cavalier cooler, holds 2 cases, and works on the honor system since it wasn't equipped with a vending mechanism, red, silver, and white, 18⅛" x 18½" x 40¾", 1940 – 1950s, EX ....$1,595.00 D

Cavalier wet box, with embossing on inside of lid and on all sides, open to the rack, white on red, EX..........$695.00 D

Cooler, lift-top fiberglas, built to resemble a Vendo V-81 vending machine, new, EX..................................$350.00 C

Glasco GBV (Glasco Bottle Vendor) dry box with slider top and front left cap catcher, Muncie, Indiana, red and white, 35½" x 20" x 40", 1950 – 1960s, EX ..... $895.00 D

Glasco single lid dry box with single hinge lid and decal lettering, white on red, 32" x 18" x 41", F .... $625.00 C

Jacobs vending machine model #26, upright shaped like a mailbox, very sought after but also the most common Jacobs machine, 1940 – 50s, red, EX ....$1,600.00 C

Vendo coin changer with keys, reproduction sign, EX, $625.00 B. *Courtesy of Muddy River Trading Co./ Gary Metz.*

Vendo model 44, restored red and white 1950s, 16" 57½" x 15½" NM, $2,400.00 I *Courtesy of Collectors Auctio Services.*

Vendo coin changer with keys and "Have a Coke" sign under glass, 12" x 15", F......................................$350.00 D

Vendo model HA56-B with front opening door, red and white, 1960s, G... $595.00 C

Vendo model #23, also known to collectors as the spin top machine, comes in standard and deluxe model, which has the silver top, vends 23 bottles and precools 7, with drop door in front for storage, 1940 – 1950s, 24" x 36" x 21", EX ....$1,395.00 D

Vendo model 83 vending machine not in great demand due in large part to the fact they are so heavy, red and white, 1940s, 32½"w x 63"h x 18"dia. G...$450.00 I

Vendo V-23, box cooler that will vend 23 bottles, made in a standard and deluxe version, fairly easy to find, 1940 – 50s, red and silver, G...........$600.00 C

Vendo V-39, a fairly common machine dispenses 39 bottles and precools 20 1940 – 1950s, 27"w x 58"h x 16"dia. NM...................................... $2,995.00 I

Salesman's sample of Westinghouse wet cooler, white on red, EX, $2,550.00 C. Back view, below, shows storage space.

Vendo model HA56-B with front opening door, red and white, 1960s, EX, $795.00 D. Courtesy of Riverside Antique Mall.

Vendo V-39, box type cooler that will vend 39 bottles and will precool slightly more than this number, 1940s, red, EX ....$675.00 C

Vendo V-59 top chest cooler, electric, dispenses 59 bottles, not very sought after by collectors, 1940s, red, EX ...$575.00 C

Vendo 81 Coca-Cola vending machine, one of the most sought after machines due in part to its compact design, original unrestored, red and white, 1950s, 27"w x 58"h x 16"dia., NM.$2,000.00 C

Vendo V-81, sought after due to its compact design and ability to dispense different size bottles, 1950s, 27" x 58" x 16", white on red, VG ....$1,300.00 C

Vendo #83 with electric coin mechanism, because of the size and weight of these machines they aren't as popular as other models, 32½" x 18" x 63", 1940 – 1950s, EX...............................$550.00 C

Vendolator 27, known as the table top, this machine would sit on a desk or special stand, dispenses 27 bottles, still fairly easy to find, 1940s, 24" x 27" x 19", red, F...............................$775.00 C

Victor C-45A salesman's sample chest cooler, cardboard, 1940 – 1950s, G, $175.00 C. Courtesy of Mitchell collection.

Vendolator 72, dual chute machine with very large embossed Coca-Cola logo, dispenses 72 and precools 6, 1950s, 25"w x 58"h x 15"d, EX, $1,500.00 D. Courtesy of Patrick's Collectibles.

Vendolator 44, upright that dispenses 44 bottles, not hard to find, 1950s, red and white, EX ....$1,200.00 B

Westinghouse model 42, embossed "Here's a Coke For You" on sides, early models were solid red, red and white, 1950s, 25"w x 53½"h x 20"dia., NM............$1,200.00 D

Westinghouse 3 Case Junior, water cooled chest box, 1940 – 1950s, red, G..$400.00 C

Westinghouse ten case Master, electric "dry" box, lid hinges in middle and opens side to side instead of front to back, cools 240 bottles, stacked, 1950s, 30½"w x 36"h x 45", NM ... $1,850.00 D

Westinghouse salesman's sample, featuring open front, white on red, VG.......................................$1,400.00 D

Coolers

Aluminum, 12 pack, 1950s, EX .$125.00 D

Floor chest, embossed lettering, yellow and white lettering on red background with bottle at left side, 29" x 32½"h x 22"dia., F...............................$475.00 D

Floor chest, embossed, yellow and white lettering on red background with bottle at left side, 29" x 32½" x 22", G ..$750.00 C

Floor chest, embossed lettering, yellow and white lettering on red background with bottle at left side, 29" x 32½"h x 22"d, VG, $950.00 B. *Courtesy of Muddy River Trading Co./Gary Metz.*

Stadium vendor, "Have a Coke," 16" x 10" x 21", VG, $195.00 C. *Courtesy of Muddy River Trading Co./Gary Metz.*

Salesman's sample sale aid shaped like box cooler, EX, $175.00 C. *Courtesy of Mitchell collection.*

Wooden cooler for iced bottles, with the original zinc lined tub, red on yellow, 1920s, 38" x 20" x 35", F, $950.00 B. *Courtesy of Muddy River Trading Co./Gary Metz.*

Glascock tabletop cooler chest type wet box, very sought after, 1930s, red and white, G .... $400.00 C
Restored, NM ....$1,600.00 C

Hemp Model 9022 picnic, white "Drink" on red, metal latch and handle, NOS, 1950s, M ....$525.00 D

Metal, Progress Refrigerator Company, Louisville, Kentucky, featuring "Things go better ..." logo embossed on front, with lift top lid, metal handles with opener under handle, white lettering on red background, F ....$125.00 D

Vinyl picnic with fishtail logo, shaped like a box with a fold-over top and strap, "Refreshing New Feeling," NM ....$50.00 D

Westinghouse Master electric chest cooler, dispenses 144 bottles, fairly common, 1930 – 1940, red, EX ....$550.00 D

Wood and metal cooler with tin sides, "Serve yourself...Please pay the clerk," 32" x 29" x 2¼", F .... $1,700.00 B

Cooler-shaped crystal with ear piece, if all parts including instructions present, increase price, EX, $225.00 C. Courtesy of Mitchell collection.

Cooler radio, prices on these vary greatly, some will go into the thousands, while others fall below the book price, remember condition, 1950s, red, VG, $850.00 C. Courtesy of Muddy River Trading Co./Gary Metz.

Boudoir, leather with gold logo at bottom, "Drink Coca-Cola So Easily Served," 1910, 3" x 8", $1,500.00 B. Courtesy of Muddy River Trading Co./Gary Metz.

Bottle radio, all original, 24", 1933, EX, $5,500.00 B. Courtesy of Muddy River Trading Co./ Gary Metz.

Bottle radio, all original, 24", 1933, G...$2,000.00 C

Bottle shaped, AM/FM, plastic, 1970s, EX ....$45.00 C

Can with the dynamic wave, 1970s, EX ....$45.00 C

Cooler design, upright, with dynamic wave, 1970s, EX ....$125.00 C

Cooler design, upright, 1980s, EX ...$75.00 C

Cooler-shaped crystal radio with ear piece, EX ....$225.00 C

Extremely rare and hard to find, radio designed to resemble an airline cooler, top lifts to reveal controls, red and white, 1950s, G ....$3,800.00 B

Vending machine design, upright, 1950s, F................................$200.00 C

Vending machine design, upright, 1960s, G ....$165.00 C

Vending machine design, upright, J. Russell, 1970s, EX .... $125.00 C

Vending machine design, upright, with dynamic wave, 1970s, EX......$125.00 C

Celluloid desk, Hilda Clark seated at table holding a glass in a holder, clock is in lower left portion of piece, working, rare and hard to find, 1901, 5½" x 7¾", EX, $8,500.00 C.

Light-up neon counter, "Pause Drink Coca-Cola," showing bottle spotlighted, restored, rare and hard to find piece, 1930s, EX, $5,500.00 C. Courtesy of Mitchell collection.

Anniversary style dome, 1950s, 3" x 5", EX ....$850.00 C

Celluloid desk, Hilda Clark seated at table holding a glass in a holder, clock is in lower left portion of piece, working, rare and hard to find, 1901, 5½" x 7¾", F .... $2,500.00 C

Counter, light-up clock, "Drink ..." is reverse painted, "Lunch with us" is painted on face, seen in several variations, red, white, green, and black, 19½" x 5" x 9", 1940s, EX ....$925.00 B

Counter, light-up, "Drink Coca-Cola Please Pay When Served," yellow numbers on black background, 19¼" x 9", VG..$775.00 C

Desk, leather composition with "Drink Coca-Cola in Bottles 5¢" at top center over clock works and smaller bottles at lower right and left corners, 1910, 4⅓" x 6", EX..............................$1,300.00 C

Dome, white lettering "Drink Coca-Cola" in red center, 1950s, 6" x 9", EX ....$1,100.00 C

Counter light-up, "Serve Yourself" base with "Drink ..." and clock on sign body, 1950s, 9" x 20", EX, $850.00 D. Courtesy of Pleasant Hill Antique Mall & Tea Room/Bob Johnson.

Telechron, red dot in hour positions with white background and white wings, 1948, 36" wing span, VG, $475.00 C Courtesy of Mitchell collection.

"Drink Coca-Cola 5¢ Delicious, Refreshing 5¢," Baird Clock Co., 15 day movement, working, 1896 – 1899, EX ....$6,500.00 B

"Drink Coca-Cola in Bottles," wooden frame, 1939 – 1940, 16" x 16", G.. $200.00 C

Glass and metal light-up clock, with red spot center, 14½" dia., EX ....$550.00 B

Light-up advertising by Modern Clock Advertising Company in Brooklyn, N.Y., aluminum case with plastic face, 1950s, 24" dia., red on white, VG..$375.00 D

Light-up, "Drink Coca-Cola in Bottles," button in center with white on red, numbers are black on white, by Swihart, 1950s, 15" dia., EX ....$400.00 D

Light-up fishtail with green background, "Drink Coca-Cola" in white lettering on red fishtail background, 1960s, VG ....$195.00 C

Light-up neon counter, "Pause Drink Coca-Cola," showing bottle spotlighted, restored, rare and hard to find piece, 1930s, EX...........................$5,500.00 C

Reverse glass metal frame clock, "Drink Coca-Cola in bottles" in red center, original jump-start motor, 1939 – 1942, EX, $550.00 B. Courtesy of Muddy River Trading Co./Gary Metz.

Round Silhouette Girl with metal frame, 1930 – 1940s, 18" dia., VG, $775.00 C. Courtesy of Mitchell collection.

Light-up round on top of rectangular shaped base, crinkle painted with the message "It's Time To Take Home A Carton," 1930 – 1940s, EX ....$5,500.00 C

Maroon, on wings with Sprite Boy on each end, it's hard to find these with wings still attached, even harder to find them with the Sprite Boy on the ends, 1950s, EX ....$850.00 C

Neon surrounded by rainbow banner from 9 to 3, "Drink Coca-Cola Sign of Good Taste" on rainbow panel, 1950s, 24" dia., NM.......................$2,700.00 C

Small china, with Coca-Cola in red on face, story is these were given to a few of the better soda fountains, G.....$3,500.00 C

Travel, German-made with brass case, 1960s, 3" x 3", G...................$135.00 C

Wall, spring-driven pendulum, "Coca-Cola, The Ideal Brain Tonic," Baird Clock Co., 1891 – 1895, 24" tall, EX.$5,000.00 B

Openers

Bakelite and metal, 1950s, black, EX ....$55.00 D

Bottle stopper and opener "Glascock Bros. Mfg. Co. Coca-Cola Quality Coolers," 1919 – 1920s, EX $85.00 D. *Courtesy of Antiques Cards and Collectibles.*

Bakelite and metal, 1950s, black, EX, $55.00 D. *Courtesy of Chief Paduke Antiques Mall.*

"Drink Bottled Coca-Cola" saber shaped opener, 1920s, EX, $200.00 C.

"Coca-Cola" block print cast iron wishbone, 1900s, EX, $120.00 D.

Bottle shaped, EX ....$50.00 C

Bottle shaped, 1950s, EX ....$150.00 C

Bottle stopper and opener, "Glascock Bros. Mfg. Co., Coca-Cola Quality Coolers," 1919 – 1920s, EX ... $85.00 D

"Coca-Cola Bottles" key style, 1930s, EX .... $55.00 C

Corkscrew, wall mounted, 1920s, EX, $85.00 C; Corkscrew, wall mounted, 1950s, EX, $35.00 C; Star opener, "Drink Coca-Cola" wall mount, 1930s, EX ....$20.00 C

"Drink Coca-Cola in Bottles" brass key, 1910s, EX.............................. $120.00 C

"Drink Coca-Cola," key-shaped with bottle cap facsimile at top, 1920 – 1950s, F................................... $40.00 C

Hand spinner, "You Pay," 1910 – 1920, EX .... $120.00 C

Metal, eagle head, "Drink Coca-Cola," engraved, 1919 – 1920s, EX ....$165.00 C

Metal, logo at end with "Drink Bottled Coca-Cola," hard-to-find, 1908, EX ....$160.00 C

Opener and spoon combination, 1930s, EX ....$130.00 D

138

Top: One blade and one opener, "Coca-Cola Bottling Company," 1910s, EX, $300.00 C.

Bottom: "The Coca-Cola Bottling Co.," blade has to be marked Kaster & Co. Coca-Cola Bottling Co., Germany, 1905 – 1915, brass, beware of reproductions, EX, $425.00 C. Courtesy of Mitchell collection.

Pearl handle with corkscrew blade and opener, 1930s, EX, $135.00 C. Courtesy of Mitchell collection.

Two blade, "Drink Coca-Cola," G, $45.00 D.

Top match pull Bakelite, rare, 1940s, EX, $1,200.00 C. Courtesy of Mitchell collection.

Knives

Bone handle, two blade, "Delicious and Refreshing," 1920, VG...........$110.00 C

Combination Henry Sears & Son, Solingen, one blade with case shaped like boot as opener, "Coca-Cola," 1920s, white, EX ....$400.00 D

'Drink Coca-Cola™ in Bottles," 1940s, EX ....$85.00 D

Pearl handle with corkscrew blade and opener, 1930s, EX .... $135.00 C

Switchblade, Remington, "Drink Coca-Cola in Bottles," 1930s, EX...$225.00 D

Truck-shaped from seminar, 1972, EX ....$35.00 D

Two blade pen knife, "Enjoy Coca-Cola," all metal, EX .... $25.00 D

Ashtrays

Ashtray with bottle lighter featuring "Drink" logo from Canadian bottler, red and white, 1950s, NM .... $250.00 B

Bronze colored, depicting 50th Anniversary in center, 1950s, EX .... $75.00 C

Ashtray, china, by the Hall China Co. This is a very rare piece. Both sides are pictured to help show both the match holder and the bottle and glass with the message "Refresh Yourself, Drink Coca-Cola," 1950, NM, $5,000.00 C. Courtesy of Charles Fletcher.

Bakelite lighter and pen holder, 1950s, EX, $185.00 C. Courtesy of Mitchell collection.

Bottle lighter, 1950s, EX, $145.00 C. Courtesy of Mitchell collection.

From Mexico, Wave logo, 1970s, EX .... $5.00 D

Glass from Dickson, Tennessee, EX ....$20.00 C

"High in energy, Low in calories," tin, 1950s, EX................................$30.00 C

Metal with molded cigarette holder, EX .... $35.00 D

Set of four, ruby red, price should be doubled if set is in original box, 1950s, EX ....$425.00 C

Top match pull Bakelite, rare, 1940s, G.. $795.00 C

Lighters

Bottle-shaped, fairly common, without the lighter it's known as "the pill box," 1950, EX ....$30.00 C

Can-shaped, with dynamic wave, M .... $40.00 C

"Drink Coca-Cola," 1950s, EX .$30.00 C

Musical, 1970s, EX................$200.00 C

Musical, red "Drink" on white dot, EX ....$155.00 D

Silver with embossed bottle, flip top, M..$45.00 D

Book, 50th Anniversary, 1936, EX, $15.00 C. *Courtesy of Mitchell collection.*

Book, "A Distinctive Drink in a Distinctive Bottle," 1922, EX, $125.00 C. *Courtesy of Mitchell collection.*

Book for Westinghouse coolers for the Bottlers of Coca-Cola, G, $8.00 C.

Paper program for the 37th National Convention in Miami, Florida, Oct. 10 – 13, 1955, American Legion, Drink Coca-Cola, 1955, VG, $40.00 C.

Matches

Book, 50th Anniversary, 1936, EX .... $10.00 C

Book from 1982 World's Fair at Knoxville, Tennessee, 1982, EX... $5.00 D

Book, "Vote for A. A. Nelson, Railroad Commissioner," VG ....$5.00 C

Book with woman on front, 1910s, VG..$95.00 C

Matchbook holder, "Compliments of The Coca-Cola Co. Coca-Cola Relieves Fatigue," 1907, EX.................$350.00 C

Matchbook holder with matches, metal, 1959, EX .... $450.00 B

Striker, "Drink Coca-Cola, Strike Matches Here," beginning to be a scarce item, 1939, red, white, and yellow, VG...$275.00 C

Coasters

"Drink Coca-Cola ice cold," with Silhouette Girl, 1940s, M ....$20.00 C

Foil, showing party tray and cooler, square, M................................. $5.00 C

Foil, showing party tray and cooler, square, M, $5.00 C. *Courtesy of Mitchell collection.*

Bottle bag, used in the days of "wet" coolers to keep the customer dry, 1931, EX, $25.00 C. *Courtesy of Mitchel collection.*

"Please put empties in the rack," green and white, M, $10.00 D. *Courtesy of Mitchell collection.*

Metal featuring the Sprite Boy, many collectors specialize in Sprite Boy items, driving the demand and value up, 1940 – 1950s, EX ....$75.00 C

Metal with likeness of Golden Gate Bridge, 4" square, 1940s, EX .....$8.00 C

Plastic with dynamic wave, "Enjoy Coca-Cola," red, 1970s, EX.... $10.00 D

"Please put empties in the rack," green and white, M ....$10.00 D

"Things go better with Coke," red and white, square with scalloped edges, M...$8.00 D

Things go better with Coke," red lettering on white background, round, M.. $8.00 D

No Drip Protectors

Bottle bag, the distinctive Coca-Cola glass, EX ....$12.00 C

Bottle protector, 1932, VG...... $15.00 C

Dispenser for no drip protectors unmarked, red, 1930s, 4½" x 8" x 2¾", EX ....$95.00 C

"In Bottles" protector, 1930 NM ....$20.00 C

Metal board with "Drink Coca-Cola" oval at top "Specials To-day," at top of writing surface, black, red, green, and yellow, 1932, EX, $450.00 D. *Courtesy of Riverside Antique Mall.*

Cardboard "Have a Coke" menu board with button at top and bottles at bottom on both sides, 1940s, VG, $225.00 C. *Courtesy of Sam and Vivian Merryman.*

Metal and wood, "Drink Coca-Cola" in white lettering inside red fishtail on green background, metal menu strips, 1950s, VG, $250.00 C. *Courtesy of Mitchell collection.*

Paper, with button sign that reads "Drink Coca-Cola Delicious and Refreshing" with graphics of man and woman at sandwich counter, message below graphics reads "Makes a light lunch refreshing," 1940s, EX............. $12.00 C

"The Pause That Refreshes," featuring three bottles, 1936, NM...........$10.00 C

Tin no drip protector dispenser with two original sleeves, in original box with mounting instructions, super find, hard to locate, 6½" x 5", EX .... $170.00 B

Menu Boards

Cardboard and wood in tin frame menu board for pricing 6½ and 12 oz. Cokes, red on black, 1950s, 25" x 15", G ... $175.00 D

Cardboard menu board, "Sign of Good Taste," with bottle on each side of board, difficult to locate in cardboard, 1959, 19" x 28" NM...............$250.00 C

Chalkboard, painted metal, made in U.S.A, American Art Works, Inc., Coshocton, Ohio, 1940, 19¼" x 27", F..$225.00 D

Heavy plastic menu board with original box and letters, clock in center, 57" x 16", 1960s, NM ....$1,000.00 B

Kay Displays, wood with metal trim, "Drink Coca-Cola," 1940s, EX, $675.00 C. Courtesy of Mitchell collection.

Great pair of nearly perfect pushes identical, with fishtail design, "Drink Coca-Cola Be Really Refreshed," 1960s, NM, $875.00 B. Courtesy of Muddy River Trading Co./Gary Metz.

Metal, painted push bar, "Drink Coca-Cola, Refresh Yourself In Bottles," with "Thanks–Call Again" on reverse, G, $375.00 C. Courtesy of Bill Mitchell.

Porcelain construction, in nearly perfect condition, "Ice Cold Coca-Cola In Bottles," 1940s – 50s, 30" wide, M, $1,000.00 B. Courtesy of Muddy River Trading Co./Gary Metz.

Kay Displays, wood and metal with button at center, 1930s, EX .... $650.00 C

Metal board with "Drink Coca-Cola" tag at top, black, red, and white, EX .....$200.00 C

Metal board with menu strips with button between the wings, 1950s, 60" x 14", NM .... $2,300.00 B

Wood and masonite Kay Displays menu board featuring a 16" button at top center, manufactured to resemble leather, 17" x 29", EX ....$525.00 B

Wood and metal Kay Displays menu board, rare and hard to find, 1940s, F ....$550.00 C

Door Pushes

Aluminum door pull, bottle shaped with "Drink" in circle overhead, aluminum and red, 1930s, NM................$275.00 D

Metal and plaster, "Drink Coca-Cola Delicious Refreshing," 1930 – 1940s, EX ....$150.00 C

Porcelain "Coke is it" with two wave logo boxes, white on red, 1970s, NM ....$95.00 B

Porcelain door plate, "Come in! Have a Coca-Cola," Canadian, yellow, white, and red, 4" x 11½", NM........ $320.00 B

Plastic bottle shaped pull for use on the newer machines, EX, $100.00 C. Courtesy of Sam and Vivian Merryman.

Left: Porcelain door pull plate, with "Pull ... Refresh Yourself," with button facsimile at bottom, green, red, and white, 4" x 8", 1950s, EX, $450.00 B. Right: Porcelain door push, "Refresh Yourself" with button artwork, green, red, and white, 4" x 8", 1950s, NM, $525.00 B.Courtesy of Muddy River Trading Co./Gary Metz.

Porcelain door push, "Thanks Call Again for a Coca-Cola," Canadian, yellow, white, and red, 3½" x 13½", NM, $325.00 B. Courtesy of Muddy River Trading Co./Gary Metz.

Porcelain "Ice Cold Coca-Cola In Bottles," 1930s, 30" x 2½", NM, $300.00 B. Courtesy of Muddy River Trading Co./Gary Metz.

Porcelain door push, Canadian, yellow and white lettering on red, 31" x 3½", EX ....$75.00 C

Porcelain door push, horizontal, "Have a Coca-Cola," yellow and white lettering on red background trimmed in yellow, 6½" x 3½", VG ....$275.00 C

Porcelain door push in French "Merci Revenez Pour un Coca-Cola," yellow, white, and red, 3½" x 13½", NM .... $160.00 B

Porcelain door push, "Take Some Coca-Cola Home Today," white lettering on red, 1950s, 34" long, NM ....$525.00 B

Porcelain door push, "Thanks Call Again for a Coca-Cola," Canadian, yellow, white, and red, 3½" x 13½", NM ....$325.00 B

Porcelain door push, "Thanks Call Again for a Coca-Cola," yellow and white lettering on red, Canadian, 1930s, EX.$235.00 C

Porcelain door push, unusual horizontal message "Prenez un Coca-Cola," yellow, white, and red, 6½" x 3¼", NM ....$120.00 B

"Refreshing Coca-Cola New Feeling," 1950 – 60s, EX......................$175.00 C

Steel with heavy paint featuring wave logo, white on black with red and white logo, 1970 – 1980s, NM.......... $75.00 B

Buddy L #5546 International in original box with all accessories, 1956, NM, $725.00 B. Courtesy of Muddy River Trading Co./Gary Metz.

Buddy L #5646 GMC with all original accessories in box, 1957, yellow, EX, $675.00 C. Courtesy of Muddy River Trading Co./Gary Metz.

Buddy L, "Enjoy Coca-Cola," complete with hand truck that mounts in side compartment, add $20.00 if MIB, 1970, EX, $95.00 C. Courtesy of Muddy River Trading Co./Gary Metz.

Tin, die cut, "Drink Coca-Cola Be Refreshed," Canadian, 1950, EX ....$300.00 C

Tin push plate with Silhouette Girl in yellow spotlight, "Drink Coca-Cola delicious refreshing," red with white and yellow lettering, 1939, 28" x 3½", NM .... $500.00 B

Trucks

Buddy L #5426, pressed steel, 1960, 15", NMIB.............................$500.00 B

Buddy L #5546 International in original box with all accessories, 1956, NM ....$725.00 B

Buddy L #5646 GMC with all original accessories in box, 1957, yellow, EX ....$675.00 C

Buddy L #5646, GMC loader with case loading line, 1950s, yellow, EX ....$450.00 C

Cargo style with working headlights and tail lights, 1950, VG .... $275.00 B

Chevy delivery, tin, Smokeyfest Estb. 1930, 1995, MIB ....$250.00 C

Corgi, Jr. featuring contour logo, 1982, NM...$35.00 D

Durham Industries van in original packaging, 1970 – 1980s, NM........$30.00 D

Buddy L Ford with original box and all accessories, 1960s, NM, $550.00 B. Courtesy of Muddy River Trading Co./Gary Metz.

Cargo style with working headlights and tail lights, 1950, EX, $350.00 C. Courtesy of Muddy River Trading Co./Gary Metz.

Gas, made in Germany, model #426-20, a rare and desirable tin wind-up litho with great detailing with a full load of tin and plastic cases, 1949, yellow, EX, $2,600.00 B. Courtesy of Muddy River Trading Co./Gary Metz.

El Camino, given away at convention in Ohio, plastic, 1995, red and white, MIB ....$20.00 C

Gas, made in Germany, model #426-20, a rare and desirable tin wind-up litho with great detailing with a full load of tin and plastic cases, 1949, yellow, EX .... $2,600.00 B

Marx, stake, yellow bed with red cab and frame with Sprite Boy decal on side of bed, 1950, G...................... $300.00 C

Marx #21 open side, 1950s, yellow, EX ....$450.00 D

Marx #1090, tin, open bed, 1956, 17", yellow and red, EX.................$450.00 B

Matchbox, tractor-trailer, Super King, 1978, NMIB ....$55.00 D

Matchbox with staggered load bed, "Drink Coca-Cola," 1960s, yellow, EX ....$155.00 D

Maxwell Co., plastic delivery van, India, 1970s, EX ....$55.00 D

Metalcraft #171 pressed steel, rubber wheels, A-frame, 1932, red and yellow, NMIB ....$2,500.00 B

Metalcraft with rubber tires, if this item were MIB price could go up by as much as $400.00, 1930s, G..............$750.00 C

147

Marx #991 with Sprite Boy decal on side, in original box, 1951, yellow, NM, $625.00 B. Courtesy of Muddy River Trading Co./Gary Metz.

Marx, plastic with original six Coca-Cola cases, Canadian, 1950s, red, EX, $525.00 B. Courtesy of Muddy River Trading Co./Gary Metz.

Marx, if in MIB condition with original box this value would nearly double, 1950, G, $275.00 C.

Metal tractor trailer with spotlight carton on the trailer, in box, but the box is a bit rough, EX ....225.00 C

Osahi, Japan, van, tin and plastic, friction, 1970s, EX..........................$85.00 C

Plastic Fun Mates from Straco, wind-up, 1970s, EX..........................$40.00 D

Plastic Marx Canadian truck with six plastic cases, wooden wheels, in original box, hard to find, red, 1950s, 11", G..........................$1,400.00 C

Renault, solid metal, 1970s, red, NM..........................$65.00 D

Rosko friction motor, beverage delivery, 1950, 8", EX..........................$475.00 C

Sanyo truck made in Japan, distributed by Allen Haddock Company in Atlanta, Georgia, with original box, battery operated, 1960s, 12½" long, EX.... $325.00 B

Siki Eurobuilt, Mack tractor trailer, die cast, 1980s, 12½", MIB ....$55.00 D

Siku-Oldtimes, metal, 1980s, 5¼", EX ....$45.00 D

Smith Miller, metal, GMC #2 of 50 stamped on bottom, with six original cases of 24 green bottles in original box, #1 is in the Smith Miller Museum, rare, 1979, red, EX ....$1,700.00 B

Clockwise, from top: Bang gun with Santa in sleigh, 1950s, M, $20.00 C.

Bang gun with clown, yellow, red, and white, 1950s, $20.00 C.

Bang gun, "It's the real thing," M, $20.00 C. Courtesy of Mitchell collection.

Bank, plastic vending machine-shaped, if found in original box value will climb to $250.00 C, 1950s, EX, $125.00 C. Courtesy of Mitchell collection.

Bank, metal, vending-shaped with coin slot on top, 1940s, 2¼" x 3", EX, $150.00 C. Courtesy of Mitchell collection.

Straco, plastic Wee People, Hong Kong, 5½", EX ....$50.00 D

Supervan, plastic, 1970s, 18" x 11", NM ....$110.00 D

Tin, even load, Japanese, 1950s, 4", yellow, EX ....$150.00 D

Tin Lineman, friction power, 1950s, VG..$200.00 D

Tin van, "Drink Coca-Cola, Delicious, Refreshing," Japanese, 1950, 4", yellow, EX ....$165.00 D

Tootsietoy van copy, die cast metal, white lettering, 1986, M...........$25.00 D

Uni Plast, Mexican #302, van with contour logo, plastic, 1978 – 1979, red, NM ....$30.00 D

Vending machine style ⅟25-scale model kit, 1970, MIB ....$75.00 C

VW van with friction motor by Taiyo, 1950s, 7½" long, VG ....$235.00 C

Winrose, Atlanta Convention, 1994, MIB ....$165.00 D

Toys

American Flyer kite, bottle at tail end of kite, 1930s, EX.......................$400.00 C

Lionel train in original box, engine has dynamic wave logo at cab, the cars advertise Fanta, Tab, Sprite, and the caboose has a large wave logo, 1970s, EX, $425.00 C. Courtesy of Sam and Vivian Merryman.

Paper mask of the likeness of Max Headroom with rubber band to hold it onto the head, 1980s, EX, $25.00 C. Courtesy of Sam and Vivian Merryman.

American Flyer train car, "Pure As Sunlight," a complete train set with track and original box would push this price to around $4,500.00, 1930s, red and green, EX ....$1,500.00 C

Ball and cap game, wooden, 1960s, EX ....$35.00 C

Bang gun with clown, yellow, red, and white, 1950s, G ....$10.00 C

Bank, cooler style, "Have a Coke" embossed in top, 1940s, 5" x 5" x 3½", EX ....$1,000.00 B

Bank, dispenser-shaped with glasses, add $200.00 if in original box, metal, 1950s, VG ....$375.00 C

Bank, metal, vending shaped with coin slot on top, 1940s, 2¼ x 3", G...$75.00 C

Bank, plastic, vending machine-shaped, 1950s, G ....$75.00 C

Barbie doll, first in Coca-Cola Fashion series, "Soda Fountain Sweetheart," styled after an advertisement in 1907, 1996, EX ....$125.00 C

Barbie doll, second in Coca-Cola Fashion series, "After the Walk," 1997, EX ....$125.00 C

Baseball glove, left-handed, MacGregor, 1970, EX, $200.00 C. Courtesy of Mitchell collection.

Yo-yo, wooden, EX, $110.00 C. Courtesy of Mitchell collection.

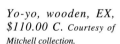

Barbie doll, third in Coca-Cola Fashion series, "Summer Daydreams," a facsimile from a 1913 Coca-Cola calendar, 1998, EX ....$125.00 C

Baseball glove, left-handed, MacGregor, 1970, EX ....$200.00 C

Baseball Hall of Fame information featuring both National and American League from 1901 to 1960, baseball-shaped, 1960, G.......................$95.00 C

Bean bag, "Enjoy Coca-Cola," with dynamic wave, 1970s, red, VG ..$30.00 C

Bicycle, EX............................$775.00 D

Boomerang, 1950s, EX ....$40.00 C

Buddy L can car, 1970s, EX ....$75.00 D

Buddy Lee doll in homemade uniform with original patches worn by "Aunt" Earlene Mitchell's father when he worked for Coca-Cola in Paducah, Kentucky, 1950s, EX ....$600.00 C

Bus, cardboard double decker with dynamic contour logo, Sweetcentre, 1980s, red, M ....$55.00 C

Caboose with wave logo, 1970s, 6½" long, EX...................................$65.00 D

Car kit, Bill Elliott's thunderboat with logo, plastic, 1:24 scale, VG ....$20.00 C

Pig bank, plastic with the message "Drink Coca-Cola Sold Everywhere," EX, $35.00 C. Courtesy of Sam and Vivian Merryman.

Train, Express Limited, still in original box with all components present, box shows a little shelf wear but nothing that detracts from the display, 1960s, EX, $450.00 C. Courtesy of Sam and Vivian Merryman.

Car, tin Taiyo Ford taxi, friction power, "Refresh With Zest," 1960s, 9", white and red, NM ....$250.00 D

Corvette, die cast, convention banquet gift, 1993, MRFB ....$35.00 C

Dart board with "Drink Coca-Cola" in center, 1950s, EX ....$95.00 D

"Express Cafe Snackbar," plastic and tin, "Drink Coca-Cola" button on front and advertisement on back, 1950 – 1960s, NM............................$175.00 C

Fanny pack, Jeff Gordon, shaped like pace car, logo, M......................$20.00 D

Friction car by Taiyo, 1960s, red and white, EX ....$250.00 B

Game box, contains two decks of 1943 cards unopened, plus marbles, dominos, chess, and checkers, 1940s, NM....................................... $475.00 D

Jump rope with whistle in one handle, "Pure as Sunlight" on other handle, 1920s, G ....$375.00 C

Kit Carson stagecoach, EX ....$150.00 C

Lionel train complete with original box and transformer, 1970s, EX ...$425.00 C

Marbles in bag that were given away with every carton, 1950, EX ....$55.00 C

Bank, truck delivery box van with dynamic wave on side, NM, $35.00 C. Courtesy of Sam and Vivian Merryman.

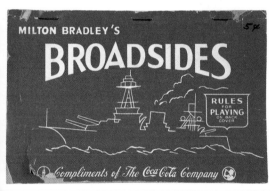

Broadsides, Milton Bradley, 1940 – 1950s, G, $125.00 C. Courtesy of Mitchell collection.

Model airplane with Coca-Cola circle for wings, 1960s, red and white, EX ....$65.00 D

Pedal car, white lettering, 1940 – 1950, 19" x 36", red, EX ....$1,300.00 B

Picnic cooler, plastic, 6", EX .$100.00 C

Play town hamburger stand made of wood, metal, and plaster in original box, very desirable piece, 1950s, EX ....$375.00 C

Puzzle, jigsaw in original can, 1960, EX ....$75.00 D

Puzzle, wire, with "Drink Coca-Cola in Bottles" on flat portion of puzzle, 1960s, EX..................................$45.00 D

Roller skates, embossed "Drink Coca-Cola in Bottles" on the face with "Pat. Aug 16, 1914" under first line, probably from the St. Louis Bottling Company, 1914, VG.............................. $900.00 B

Shopping basket, child's size with grocery graphics printed on both sides of basket liner, complete with contents, 1950s, EX...............................$425.00 C

Stove, "Drink Coca-Cola with Your Meals," 1930s, green, EX ...$2,200.00 C

Tic-Tac-Toe with bottle pawns, 1950s, EX ....$125.00 C

Flip game, early, showing boy drinking from a bottle with a straw, 1910 – 1920s, VG, $875.00 C. Courtesy of Mitchell collection.

Flying disc, plastic with dynamic wave logo on top, "Coke adds life to having fun," 1960s, EX, $12.00 C. Courtesy of Mitchell collection.

Top, plastic, "Coke Adds Life To…Fun Times," 1970s, VG...................$20.00 C

Train tank car HO gauge, "Enjoy Coca-Cola," 1980s, G........................$25.00 C

Whistle, plastic, "Merry Christmas Coca-Cola Bottling, Memphis, Tennessee, 1950, EX.....................$30.00 C

Whistle, thimble-shaped, 1940s, EX ....$70.00 C

Whistle, tin, "Drink Coca-Cola," 1930, red and yellow, VG ....$135.00 D

Whistle, wood, "Drink Coca-Cola," 1940s, EX.................................$80.00 D

Yo-yo, Russell Championship, "Drink Coca-Cola" on side, 1960, EX.$45.00 D

Yo-yo, wooden, VG ....$125.00 C

Games

1943, EX ....$210.00 C

Baseball bat, 1950s, EX ....$175.00 C

Baseball bat, wooden, featuring Coca-Cola at end, 1968, EX..............$55.00 D

Baseball glove, left-handed, 1920s, EX ....$350.00 C

Game in original cardboard box, contains table tennis, bingo, dominos, two decks of cards, chess, checkers, 1940s, EX, $1,150.00 D. Courtesy of Antiques, Cards and Collectibles/Ray Pelley.

Dynamic wave trademark, 1985, M, $20.00 D.

Girl sitting in field, 1974, M, $20.00 D.

Betty, 1977, M............................$30.00 C

Bingo card, "Drink Coca-Cola" in center spot, 1950s, EX...................$20.00 D

Bingo card with slide covers, "Play Refreshed Drink Coca-Cola From Sterilized Bottles," 1930s, EX.......$55.00 D

Bottle and food, 1974, M ....$25.00 C

Broadsides, Milton Bradley, 1940 – 1950s, F....................................$75.00 D

Broadsides, Milton Bradley, 1940 – 1950s, EX..............................$150.00 C

Canned Wizzer Coke game, EX...$10.00 D

Checkers, dominos, cribbage board, two decks of cards, and a bridge score pad in a carrying box, 1940s, VG......$200.00 D

Checkers, wooden, Coca-Cola name in script on top, 1940 – 1950s, EX....$45.00 C

Chinese Checkers board with Silhouette Girl logo, 1930 – 1940s, EX....$95.00 D

"Coke Is It," 1985, M............... $25.00 C

Cribbage board, 1940s, EX......$60.00 D

Dart board, 1940s, EX............$100.00 C

Dart board, 1950s, EX ....$55.00 D

Playing cards, complete with Joker and Bridge scoring cards, featuring girl with bottle, 1928, NM, $2,500.00 B. Courtesy of Muddy River Trading Co./Gary Metz.

"Coca-Cola adds life to everything nice," 1976, M, $30.00 C.

Girl at beach, 1956, M, $85.00 C.

Dart set of three darts, 1940 – 1950s, EX ....$125.00 C

Dominos, wooden in original box, 1940 – 1950s, VG ....$50.00 D

"Drink Coca-Cola In Bottles," 1938, M ....$135.00 C

Flying disc, plastic with dynamic wave logo on top, "Coke adds life to having fun," 1960s, NM......................$15.00 C

Football, miniature, 1960s, black and white, EX ....$10.00 D

Game box, contains two decks of 1943 cards unopened, plus marbles, dominos, chess, and checkers, 1940s, NM.......................................$475.00 D

Game in original cardboard box, contains table tennis, bingo, dominos, two decks of cards, chess, and checkers, 1940s, EX........................... $1,200.00 D

Game of Steps to Health, based on the Malden Health Series, cardboard tri-fold board game, prepared and distributed by The Coca-Cola Company of Canada, Limited, 1940 – 1950s, EX ......$135.00 C

Playing cards, friends and family, 1980, M, $55.00 C.

Kansas City Spring Fling '82, M, $55.00 C. Courtesy of Mitchell collection.

Girl sitting in field, 1974, M ....$20.00 D

Horse Race, in original box, EX ....$350.00 C

Lady at party with a bottle, 1951, M..$80.00 C

Magic kit, 1965, EX...............$175.00 D

Playing cards, Arkansas Chapter "Holiday Happening" in plastic, 1995, EX $35.00

Playing cards, Atlanta Christmas, 1992, EX ....$50.00 D

Playing cards, Atlanta Christmas, 1993, EX ....$45.00 D

Playing cards, Atlanta, Ga. convention cards, 1990s, NRFB ....$30.00 D

Playing cards, Beach scene, 1960, M...$95.00 D

Playing cards, bottle on ice man, 1958, M..$85.00 C

Playing cards, "Coca-Cola adds music to my life," 1988, EX...............$50.00 D

Playing cards, "Coke Refreshes You Best," 1961, M.......................$70.00 C

Military nurse in uniform, 1943, EX, $135.00 C. Courtesy of Mitchell collection.

Woman in circle, 1943, M, $100.00 C. Courtesy of Mitchell collection.

Playing cards, couple playing tennis, 1979, M ....$45.00 D

Playing cards, couple sitting and resting under tree in planter, 1963, M ...$100.00 C

Playing cards, Dearborn Convention, 1993, EX ....$35.00 D

Playing cards, "Drink Coca-Cola," party scene, 1960, M.................$75.00 D

Playing cards, Elaine, 1915, EX ....$1,150.00 C

Playing cards featuring a Coca-Cola bottle, 1963, white and red, EX .....$40.00 D

Playing cards featuring the bobbed hair girl, "Refresh Yourself," in original box, 1928, EX ....$600.00 C

Playing cards, friends and family, 1980, M...$55.00 D

Playing cards from Campbellsville, Ky. Bottling Co., G ....$50.00 C

Playing cards from the California Chapter of the Cola Clan, 1986, EX ....$125.00 D

Playing cards, girl in circle surrounded by leaves, in original box, 1943, EX ....$105.00 D

Spotter lady, 1943, M, $125.00 C.
Courtesy of Mitchell collection.

Score keeper, cardboard, keeps score of runs, hits, and errors by both teams, by score wheels, 1900s, VG, $135.00 C. Courtesy of Mitchell collection.

Playing cards, girl in pool, "Sign of Good Taste," 1959, EX ....$80.00 D

Playing cards, Kansas City Convention, 1995, NRFB ....$25.00 C

Playing cards, Kansas City Spring Fling, 1993, EX......................$65.00 D

Playing cards, Louisville, Ky. convention, 1980s, NRFB ....$22.00 C

Playing cards, model that was used on 1923 calendar, 1977, M ....$50.00 D

Playing cards, "Refreshing New Feeling," featuring couple in front of fireplace, 1963, M........................$80.00 C

Playing cards, Smokeyfest Chapter, 1994, EX ....$30.00 C

Playing cards, Smokeyfest Chapter, 1995, EX ....$35.00 C

Playing cards, snowman in a bottle cap hat, 1959, M ....$85.00 D

Playing cards, woman with tray of bottles, 1963, M............................$60.00 C

Pool cue, dynamic wave logo, EX ....$60.00 C

Pool cue with dynamic contour logo, EX ....$40.00 D

"Drink Coca-Cola in Bottles," 1938, green wheat, EX, $150.00 C. Courtesy of Mitchell collection.

Woman in uniform with wings below photo, 1943, EX, $150.00 C. Courtesy of Mitchell collection.

Poster puzzle with scenes from various cardboard posters, mounted on board, 35" x 43", VG....................... $100.00 C

Puzzle in original box with a Coke girl on front enjoying a glass of Coke, 500 pieces, G.....................$75.00 C

Puzzle in original box with graphics of young lovers in front of an old general store with an early Coke cooler, 1000 pieces, EX ....$25.00 C

Puzzle, jigsaw, "An Old Fashioned Girl," in original box, 1970 – 1980s, NM..$20.00 D

Puzzle, jigsaw, Coca-Cola Pop Art, in sealed can, 1960, NM..............$25.00 C

Puzzle, jigsaw, Hawaiian beach, rare, in original box, NM...................$165.00 C

Puzzle, jigsaw, in original box, "Crossing The Equator," NM ....$135.00 D

Puzzle, jigsaw, Teen Age Party, NM...$75.00 D

Puzzle, wooden blocks that spell "Ice Cold Coca-Cola," 15", NM.......................................$300.00 D

Case, snap lid with raised bottle in center, all metal, EX, $85.00 C.

Cuff links, gold finish, "Enjoy Coca-Cola," glass-shaped, 1970s, EX, $55.00 C. Courtesy of Mitchell collection.

Money clip, compliments of Coca-Cola Bottling Works, Nashville, Tenn., EX, $55.00 C. Courtesy of Mitchell collection.

Record chart, baseball-shaped, National League Hall of Fame, 1960, EX.$155.00 D

Red and white, 1986, M ....$25.00 C

"Refresh," 1958, M ....$85.00 C

Ring toss game with Santa Claus at top of handle, VG...........................$35.00 D

Score keeper, cardboard, keeps score of runs, hits, and errors by both teams, by score wheels, 1900s, VG........$135.00 C

Shanghai, MIB ....$20.00 D

Steps to Health with original playing pieces and envelope, 1938, 11" x 26", NM ....$145.00 D

Tower of Hanoi, EX...............$225.00 D

Jewelry

Belt and buckle, "All Star Dealer Campaign Award," 1950 – 1960s, M ..$35.00 D

Brooch, "Drink Coca-Cola," EX ..$40.00 D

Case, snap lid with raised bottle in center, all metal, EX ....$85.00 C

Coca-Cola Bottlers convention pin, shield-shaped, 1912, EX ....$500.00 D

Coca-Cola Bottling Company annual convention pin, 1915, red, white, blue, EX ....$600.00 D

Coca-Cola Bottling Company annual convention pin, 1916, EX ......$600.00 D

Charm bracelet with bottle and glass charms, EX, $130.00 C. Courtesy of Mitchell collection.

Bottle earrings still on display card, NM, $20.00 C. Courtesy of Sam and Vivian Merryman.

Tie tack, 30-year service award, still in box, NM, $45.00 C. Courtesy of Sam and Vivian Merryman.

Coca-Cola 100th anniversary wrist watch, featuring a diamond chip at 12 o'clock, NM ....$120.00 B

Cufflinks, gold finish, "Enjoy Coca-Cola," glass-shaped, 1970s, EX. $65.00 C

Match safes, for wood matches, "Drink Coca-Cola," F........................$175.00 C

Money clip, "Coca-Cola" in white lettering on gold plate, EX ....$30.00 C

Money clip, compliments of Coca-Cola Bottling Works, Nashville, Tenn., EX .... $55.00 C

Money clip, gold plate with "Drink Coca-Cola" button in center, F.............$35.00 C

Money clip, silver plate, "Enjoy Coca Cola," dynamic wave with knife VG.. $30.00 C

Necklace with bottle, EX ....$85.00 C

Raquel Welch bracelet, EX ......$50.00 C

Service pin, 5 year, EX ....$75.00 C

Service pin, 10 year, EX ....$85.00 C

Service pin, 15 year, EX ....$90.00 C

Service pin, 20 year, EX ....$95.00 C

Service pin, 30 year, EX ....$135.00 D

Service pin, 50 year, as you might expect this pin is hard to find and i extremely rare, EX ....$425.00 C

Apron, cloth, "Be Really Refreshed" with button on chest portion, 1950s, white, VG, $35.00 C. *Courtesy of Mitchell collection.*

Uniform pants and shirt, green with wave patch over pocket, EX, $65.00 C. *Courtesy of Sam and Vivian Merryman.*

Driver's cap with hard bill, red, white, and yellow, 1930s, EX, $95.00 C. *Courtesy of Mitchell collection.*

Cowboy hat; this item was an employee incentive award item, still in original box in unused condition, NM, $150.00 C. *Courtesy of Sam and Vivian Merryman.*

Tie clasp with bottle on chain, 1940s, VG... $40.00 D

Watch fob, brass swastika (this was a good luck symbol until the 1930s when the Nazi connection made it an ugly form), 1920s, EX....................$175.00 C

Watch fob, brass with gold wash, "Relieves Fatigue" on front, "Drink Coca-Cola Sold Everywhere 5¢" on back, 1907, EX.......................$165.00 C

Clothing

Backpack, "Official soft drink of the 1984 Olympics," never used, 1984, EX..$20.00 C

Belt, web construction with metal slide buckle that has graphics of the dynamic wave on the front, and the message "Enjoy Coke," 1960s, NM.......$20.00 C

Belt, web construction with metal slide buckle trimmed in red outline with the message "Enjoy Coke," NM ....$15.00 C

Bowler's shirt, red and white, "Things go better with Coke," 1960s, EX ....$30.00 C

Brown uniform necktie with dynamic wave squares, EX.....................$12.00 C

Cap, felt beanie, 1930 – 1940s, 8" dia., VG... $45.00 C

Left: Leather black, 1920s, EX $100.00 C.

Right: Leather, "Drink Coca-Cola, Delicious Refreshing," 1920s, EX $85.00 C. Courtesy of Mitchell collection.

Suspenders, white with red lettering that carries the message "Enjoy Coke," with metal snap closures, these were company issued to employees, NM, $35.00 C. Courtesy of Sam and Vivian Merryman.

Coin purse with snap closures, leather, arrow, "Whenever you see an arrow think of Coca-Cola," 1909, VG, $175.00 C. Courtesy of Mitchell collection.

Uniform shirt, short sleeve, 1960s, VG, $60.00 C. Courtesy of Mitchell collection.

Coke uniform with round drink patch, 38 regular, VG........................$125.00 C

Drawstring "it's the real thing" pants, EX...$15.00 C

Driver's cap with hard bill, red, white, and yellow, 1930s, EX .... $95.00 C

Driver's cap with round "Drink" patch and hard bill, hats like this are becoming hard to locate, EX ....$125.00 C

Driver's folding cap, 1950s, VG.$70.00 C

Uniform coat, brown with red and square dynamic wave logo patch, nicknamed the hunting coat, original Riverside manufacturer's tag, EX ....$55.00 C

Uniform pants and shirt, green with wave patch over pocket, EX ....$65.00 C

Uniform shirt, short sleeve, 1960s. VG...$60.00 C

Uniform vest, quilted with square wave patch, original Riverside tag, EX ....$35.00 C

Vest for company uniform, large "Drink ... in bottles" on back and smaller round "Drink" patch over left pocket, EX ....$65.00 C

Bottle hanger, Santa Claus in refrigerator full of bottles being surprised by small child, 1950s, EX, $35.00 C. Courtesy of Mitchell collection.

Plastic, "Enjoy Coca-Cola," 1960s, black, EX, $15.00 C. Courtesy of Mitchell collection.

Cardboard cut out, Santa Claus, "Greetings from Coca-Cola," 1946, 6" x 12", EX, $225.00 C. Courtesy of Mitchell collection.

Cardboard stand up Santa Claus holding three bottles in each hand with a button behind Santa, 1950s, VG, $200.00 C. Courtesy of Mitchell collection.

Wallets

Coin purse with gold lettering engraved in leather "When thirsty try a bottle," "Coca-Cola Bottling Company" with a paper label bottle to the left of lettering, 1907, maroon, EX ....$100.00 C

Coin purse with snap closures, leather, arrow, "Whenever you see an arrow think of Coca-Cola," 1909, VG..$175.00 C

Coin purse with snap closure top, leather, reads "Compliments of Coca-Cola Bottling Co., Memphis, Tenn.," 1910 – 1920s, VG .... $185.00 C

Leather, "Drink Coca-Cola, Delicious, Refreshing," 1920s, EX .... $85.00 C

Tri-fold with calendar, leather with gold embossed lettering, 1918, black, EX ....$85.00 C

Santas

Cardboard cut out, "Free Decorations in cartons of Coke," Santa standing on ladder in front of Christmas tree with a small girl on stool at bottom of ladder, 1960s, EX................................$30.00 C

Cardboard cut out, Santa Claus in front of an open refrigerator door holding a bottle, this folds in the middle, easel-back, 1948, 5' tall, F...............$235.00 C

Display topper, cardboard, "Stock up for the Holidays," Santa holding a bottle behind a six pack, 1950s, EX, $150.00. Courtesy of Mitchell collection.

Cardboard easel back Santa cutout, message reads, "Host for the Holidays ... Take enough Coke Home," 1952, 13" x 24", EX, $500.00 B. Courtesy of Muddy River Trading Co./Gary Metz.

Porcelain, large Santa holding a bottle and a string of lights standing beside a small wooden stool with a striped package sitting on the top step, new, EX, $145.00 C. Courtesy of Mitchell collection.

Cardboard cut out, "Things go better with Coke," Santa and little boy with dog, 1960s, 36", G.....................$30.00 C

Cardboard die cut hanging sign "Christmas Greetings," 1932, NM .....$4,200.00 B

Cardboard poster with graphics of Santa holding a bottle of Coke, 1940s, 43" x 32", EX................................$1,000.00 B

Cardboard Santa Claus Santa Packs blank price sign, NOS, NM..... $35.00 C

Cardboard Santa hanger, "Add Zest to the Season," Canadian, 1949, 10½" x 18½", EX .... $900.00 B

Cardboard stand up Santa Claus resting one arm on a post while holding a bottle with the other, a holly Christmas wreath is shown in the rear, 1960s, EX........$95.00 C

Cardboard truck sign featuring Santa with both hands full of Coke bottles "Santa's Helpers," 1960s, 66" x 32", G.......$125.00 B

Carton stuffer Santa Claus, "Good taste for all," VG ....$50.00 D

Doll, Rushton, holding a bottle, 1960s, 16" high, EX..........................$145.00 C

Paper hanger, Season's Greetings with Santa and helicopter, 1962, 16" x 24", NM ....$425.00 B

Royal Orleans porcelain figurine featuring Santa hushing a small dog and holding a bottle, one in a limited six-part series, 1980, EX, $140.00 C. Courtesy of Mitchell collection.

Birthday card for Coca-Cola employees featuring the Sprite Boy, the message reads "A Treat in store...for your Birthday," unused, EX, $20.00 C. Courtesy of Sam and Vivian Merryman.

Cardboard die cut of Sprite Boy with bottle cap hat presenting an icy cup of Coke, 37½" x 29", EX, $250.00 C. Courtesy of Sam and Vivian Merryman.

Cardboard, die cut, Sprite Boy sign featuring a six pack, 34" x 43", G, $375.00 C.

Paper sign designed for pole mount display with graphics of Santa and information about receiving a collectible Santa Cola cup, 22" x 30", NM ....$15.00 C

Poster, cardboard, "A Merry Christmas calls for Coke," Santa seated in green easy chair while elves bring him food, 1960s, 16" x 24", VG ....$65.00 C

Poster, cardboard, "Coke adds life to Holiday Fun," lettering on sign in front of Santa, 1960s, EX ....$45.00 D

Poster, cardboard, "Coke adds life to Holiday Fun," lettering on sign in front of Santa, 1960s, G ....$30.00 C

Poster cardboard, "Coke adds life to Holiday Fun," with artwork of Santa holding list and bottle, 1960s, 36" x 20", EX.....................................$95.00 C

Poster, cardboard, "Extra Bright Refreshment" Santa beside a Christmas tree with a six pack in front, 1955, 16" x 27", EX.....................................$85.00 C

Poster, cardboard, "Real holidays call for the real thing," Santa holding a Christmas wreath, 1970s, 36" tall, EX .... $35.00 D

Poster, cardboard, "Real holidays call for the real thing," Santa holding a Christmas wreath, 1970s, 36" tall, G...$20.00 C

167

Cardboard poster, featuring Sprite Boy displaying two bottle sizes, 1955, 16" x 27", NM, $225.00 C. *Courtesy of Muddy River Trading Co./Gary Metz.*

Cardboard cut out sign featuring Sprite Boy and Santa Claus with reindeer, has original easel back attachment, 1940s, 26" x 52", EX, $525.00 B. *Courtesy of Muddy River Trading Co./Gary Metz.*

Cardboard, "Have a Coke," sign featuring Sprite Boy advertising King Size, has a hanger and easel back attachment, 1957, 18" square, EX, $170.00 B. *Courtesy of Muddy River Trading Co./Gary Metz.*

Hat, soda person, paper fold-up, featuring Sprite Boy, 1950s, VG, $30.00 C. *Courtesy of Mitchell collection.*

Royal Orleans porcelain figurine with Santa holding a book in front of a fireplace that has a bottle on the mantel, part of a limited six-part series, all six pieces together MIB $1,500.00, 1980s, EX ....$130.00 C

Sign, cardboard, double sided hanging, "Things go better with Coke," Santa and a couple kissing, 1960, 13½" x 16", EX .... $55.00 C

Sign, cardboard rocket, "Drink Coca-Cola Festive Holidays," die cut dimensional Santa, 1950s, 33" tall, EX ....$375.00 D

Sign, cardboard, "Santa's Helpers," Santa holding six bottles, 1950s, VG..$110.00 D

Sprite Boy

1945 pocket calendar, with Sprite Boy looking around bottle on left side, EX ....$55.00 C

Blotter, 1947, EX ....$95.00 B

Cardboard, case insert with Sprite Boy, "Take some home," 10" x 13", 1944, NM ....$220.00 B

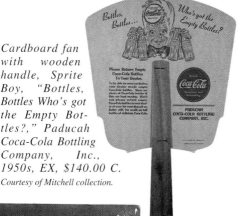

Cardboard fan with wooden handle, Sprite Boy, "Bottles, Bottles Who's got the Empty Bottles?," Paducah Coca-Cola Bottling Company, Inc., 1950s, EX, $140.00 C. *Courtesy of Mitchell collection.*

Napkin holder with Sprite Boy panel on side, "Have a Coke 5¢," 1950, VG, $725.00 C. *Courtesy of Gary Metz.*

Paper tablet, "Safety ABC's," with graphics of the Sprite Boy in bottle cap hat, EX, $18.00 C. *Courtesy of Sam and Vivian Merryman.*

Cardboard fold out fan with Sprite Boy from the Coca-Cola bottler at Memphis, Tennessee, 1951, F .... $65.00 C

Cardboard, horizontal poster, featuring Sprite Boy advertising family size too, in original wooden frame, 1955, 36" x 20", EX .... $550.00 B

Cardboard poster, featuring Sprite Boy and a six pack, probably part of another larger sign, 41½" x 27½", 1946, EX .... $525.00 B

Cardboard, promotional sign for cups featuring Sprite Boy, 1940s, 15" x 12", F .... $375.00 D

Cardboard sign, "Now Family Size too!," Sprite Boy advertising Coca-Cola all on yellow background, 1955, 16" x 27", EX .... $195.00 C

Cardboard sign, Sprite Boy advertising the ice cold 12 oz. king size bottle, 1957, M .... $400.00 C

Glass sign, decal mounted on glass and framed, Sprite Boy, advertising bottles sales, note bottle cap hat as opposed to fountain hat, 13" x 13", NM .... $425.00 D

"Have a Coke" coaster with Sprite Boy, 1940s, M .... $15.00 C

Marx #991, pressed steel truck, Sprite Boy decal, 1950s, gray, MIB . $1,000.00 D

169

Wood and masonite, Kay Displays sign advertising Sundaes and Malts with 12" button in center and Sprite Boy on each end, 1950s, 6'6" x 1', NM, $1,050.00 B. Courtesy of Muddy River Trading Co./Gary Metz.

Wood, Sprite Boy, Welcome Friend, 1940, 32" x 14", EX, $550.00 C. Courtesy of Mitchell collection.

Wood Kay Displays sign with a 12" button in center of two wings that has graphics of Sprite Boy at each end with a bottle of Coke, 1940s, 3' x 1', NM, $1,300.00 B. Courtesy of Muddy River Trading Co./Gary Metz.

Metal button sign, 12", with wings, Sprite Boy on ends and lettering of Sundaes and Malts in between, 1950s, 12" x 78", F.....................................$600.00 D

Napkin with Sprite Boy, 1950s, M..$18.00 D

National Geographic, back cover, "Travel Refreshed" with Santa and Sprite Boy, 6⅞" x 10", 1949, G .... $12.00 C

Paper, "Come In, Have a Coke," framed under glass, F ....$95.00 D

Paper, "Come in … we have Coca-Cola 5¢," Sprite Boy with glasses, 1944, 25" x 8", VG ....$350.00 B

Paper, "We have Coca-Cola 5¢," Sprite Boy, rare, soda fountain hat on Sprite Boy, 1944, 22" x 7", NM........$600.00 C

Paper window sign with graphics of Sprite Boy with bottle cap hat advertising "6 bottles 25¢," still has original stick-ons, probably NOS, 1950, 25" x 10", NM................................$300.00 B

Porcelain, "Buvez Coca-Cola," with Sprite Boy in spotlight, French, 1940s, 58" x 18", EX ....$750.00 B

Porcelain, single sided Sprite Boy sign with spotlight on boy, French, white and yellow on red, 17½" x 54", 1954, EX ....$210.00 B

Paper, Sprite Boy, "Come In Have a Coke," framed under glass, EX, $175.00 C. Courtesy of Mitchell collection.

Tin, round button Sprite Boy sign with bottle and button, embossed edge, string hung, 1940s, 12¾" dia., EX, $775.00 C.

Two-sided, "The Pause that Refreshes," five-piece, 1930s, VG, $775.00 B. Courtesy of Muddy River Trading Co./Gary Metz.

Sprite Boy coloring book, issued by the Coca-Cola bottling plant in Gulfport, Mississippi, with pages that promote Coke, Tab, Mello-Yello, and Fanta, 22 pages, 1980s, EX......................$10.00 C

Sprite Lucky Lymon, talking vinyl figure holding a can of Sprite, says "I like the way you make me laugh, I like the Sprite in you," a West Coast offering and hard to find, 7" tall, NM....$10.00 C

Tin, rack sign with Sprite Boy decal, red background, 16" x 23", 1940 – 1950s, EX..............................$300.00 B

Festoons

Autumn Leaves, five-piece festoon, designed for use on a soda fountain back bar, 1927, G .... $1,000.00 C

Cardboard, "Balloons" featuring couple in clowns suits, hard to find item, 1912, EX ....$5,600.00 C

Heavy stock paper, framed and matted under glass, 96" x 20", 1918, EX ....$4,500.00 B

Lily Pads festoon, five-piece, 1935, EX ....$2,600.00 B

Locket, five pieces with original envelope, 1939, NM ....$1,800.00 C

Five-piece Square Dance back bar display with the original envelope, 1957, 18" x 11', G, $1,400.00 B. *Courtesy of Gary Metz.*

Nine-piece back bar display, hard to find, complete with original envelope and instruction card, 1958, 12' long, NM, $1,600.00 B. *Courtesy of Muddy River Trading Co./Gary Metz.*

Masonite three-piece festoon with the message "howdy partner ... pause ... refresh," EX .... $850.00 B

Parasols, five-piece festoon, originally placed on a soda fountain back bar, 1927, G ....$4,700.00 B

People in period dress from 1886 to 1951, 1951, NM ....$1,200.00 B

State tree complete with original display envelope, 1950s, EX .... $750.00 C

Swan, five pieces with original envelope, 1938, EX ....$1,800.00 C

Three pieces of a five-piece back bar display featuring girls' heads, 1951, VG..$900.00 C

Verbena, center piece only shown, price is for complete five-piece set with ribbons, VG.......................$1,500.00 B

Wood flower, three pieces with original envelope, 1934, NM............$1,800.00 C

Wooden, three-piece Kay Displays made of plywood and metal, featuring embossed icicles, displayed at Weidelich Pharmacies until it closed in the early 1960s, 1936, 36" x 20" center, 36" x 18" end pieces, G ....$4,000.00 B

Dispenser with porcelain base, frosted glass body and lid, white lettering on red base, 1920s, 17" tall, NM, $6,200.00 B. *Courtesy of Muddy River Trading Co./Gary Metz.*

Plastic toy dispenser, played with but still has all the original parts, red and white, 1970s, VG, $110.00 C.

Cup dispenser of heavy metal construction in triangle shape, 26" tall, EX, $425.00 B. *Courtesy of Muddy River Trading Co./Gary Metz.*

Plastic and metal, three-head dispenser for Sprite and Coke, "Have a Coke" on side, red and white, VG, $275.00 D.

Wooden, three-piece set manufactured by Kay Displays, 1930s, 37" x 10" center, 9" x 11½" end pieces, NM ....$2,800.00 B

Dispensers

Counter dispenser, bolt-on, 1940 – 1950s, VG ....$750.00 D

Dispenser, plastic "Drink Coca-Cola" with dynamic wave logo on tank, 1970s, red and white, EX........$50.00 D

Dispenser, toy, with original glasses, "Drink Coca-Cola," 1950s, EX ....$175.00 C

Dole countertop dispenser, white and red, 14½" x 11½" x 25", G ... $675.00 B

Plastic and metal, three-head dispenser for Sprite and Coke, "Have a Coke" on side, red and white, VG ....$275.00 D

Plastic toy dispenser, played with but still has all the original parts, red and white, 1970s, VG...................$110.00 C

Syrup dispenser, ceramic, complete, marked "The Wheeling Pottery Co.," 1896, VG........................... $5,500.00 B

Syrup dispenser, reproduction made of hard rubber, 1950s, EX ....$350.00 B

Axe, *"For Sportsmen" "Drink Coca-Cola," 1930, EX, $1,050.00 C. Courtesy of Mitchell collection.*

Bookmark, paper, *"Drink Coca-Cola Delicious and Refreshing" featuring Lillian Nordica at stand table with a glass, 1900s, 2¼" x 5¼", NM, $1,500.00 B. Courtesy of Muddy River Trading Co./Gary Metz.*

45rpm record, *Trini Lopez, with dust cover advertising Fresca, 1967, EX, $25.00 C. Courtesy of Mitchell collection.*

Miscellaneous

Astro-Float mounts on top of bottle, designed to put ice cream in for a Coke float or ice to help cool down your drink, 1960s, VG .... $30.00 C

Axe, "For Sportsmen" "Drink Coca-Cola," 1930, G .... $750.00 C

Badge holder, Bottler's Conference, metal and celluloid, 1943, EX..$65.00 C

Bell, stamped metal, "Refresh Yourself Drink Coca-Cola In Bottles" on both sides, 1930s, 3¼" tall, NM.....$500.00 B

Bolo tie, Kit Carson, neckerchief in original mailer envelope, 1950s, EX ....$95.00 C

Bookmark, celluloid oval, "What Shall We Drink? Drink Coca-Cola 5¢," 1906, 2" x 2¼", EX........................$750.00 C

Bookmark, celluloid, "Refreshing Drink Coca-Cola Delicious 5¢," 1900s, 2" x 2¼", EX ....$1,800.00 C

Bookmark, plastic with wave logo, 1970, white and red, EX.............$5.00 C

Bottle lamp, with cap and original marked brass base, very rare and highly desirable, 1920s, 20", NM.....$7,200.00 B

Bowl, green, scalloped edge Vernonware, "Drink Coca-Cola Ice Cold," 1930s, green, EX, $450.00 C. *Courtesy of Muddy River Trading Co./Gary Metz.*

"Coke" sandwich toaster with original cord, 1930s, VG, $1,500.00 B. *Courtesy of Muddy River Trading Co./Gary Metz.*

Bookmark, celluloid, "Refreshing Drink Coca-Cola Delicious 5¢," 1900s, 2" x 2¼", F, $500.00 C. Courtesy of Riverbend Auction Company.

Bowl, green, scalloped edge Vernonware, "Drink Coca-Cola Ice Cold," 1930s, green, EX .... $450.00 C

Box of straws, with graphics of Coke bottle on all four sides, and the message "The pause that Refreshes," 1930s, EX ....$575.00 B

Brass bookends in shape of bottle, 1960s, EX............................ $225.00 B

Bumper sticker, "America – You're the real thing," EX ....$5.00 C

Bumper sticker, extolling the advantages of safe driving because of Coca-Cola, EX....................................$5.00 C

Cardboard display of Coca-Cola bottling plant in San Diego, note the streamline architecture; this has been designated a historic cultural monument, 14" x 4½" x 6½", EX.....$75.00 B

Card table with bottle in each corner, advertisement sheet under side of table boasts of the fact it's so strong it can hold an adult standing on it, 1930, VG..$275.00 C

Cash register topper, "Please Pay When Served," light-up, 1950s, EX..........$950.00 B

Chewing gum display box, held twenty 5¢ packages, cardboard, rare, 1920s, VG....................................$1,500.00 B

Brass book ends in shape of bottles, 1960s, EX, $225.00 B. Courtesy of Gene Harris Antique Auction Center, Inc.

Box of straws that carries the message "Be really refreshed," 1960s, 8½" tall, EX, $250.00 B. Courtesy of Muddy River Trading Co./Gary Metz.

Bottle lamp, with cap and original marked brass base, very rare and highly desirable, 1920s, 20", NM, $7,200.00 B. Courtesy of Muddy River Trading Co./Gary Metz.

Chewing gum jar with thumb nail type lid, 1930s, M ....$500.00 D

Cigar band, 1930, EX ....$165.00 D

Cigarette box, 50th Anniversary frosted glass, 1936, VG.....................$625.00 C

"Coke" sandwich toaster with original cord, 1930s, F........................$750.00 C

Cone cup, waxed cardboard with the message "Drink Coca-Cola" on the side, EX....................................$12.00 C

Cup, paper, red lettering "Things Go Better With Coke" on white square, 1960s, NM ....$8.00 D

Dialing finger, "It's the real thing," 1970s, EX................................$15.00 D

Display bottle, hard rubber, 1948, 4' tall, EX ....$975.00 D

Door lock, metal, "Drink Coca-Cola in Bottles, Delicious and Refreshing," 1930s, EX................................$75.00 C

"Drink Coca-Cola" with net end, EX ....$20.00 C

Dust cover, Lone Ranger, 1971, EX ....$40.00 D

Fact wheel, United States at a glance, EX .... $95.00 C

Cigarette box, 50th Anniversary frosted glass, 1936, EX, $700.00 C.
Courtesy of Mitchell collection.

Box of straws, with graphics of Coke bottle on all four sides, and the message "The Pause that Refreshes," 1930s, EX, $575.00 B. Courtesy of Muddy River Trading Co./Gary Metz.

Fence post topper made from heavy cast iron, used to decorate fence pillars outside bottling plants, has a threaded base, 20" tall, EX ....$500.00 D

Flashlight in original box, 1980, EX ....$40.00 D

Fly swatters, "Drink Coca-Cola In Bottles," EX..................................$95.00 D

Glass negative for the 1940s poster featuring the tennis girl, very unusual and rare, 20" x 24", G ....$110.00 D

Globe, leaded glass, round, "Coca-Cola," rare, 1920s, EX ......$10,000.00 D

Globe, milk glass, from ceiling fixture, "Drink Coca-Cola," 1930 – 1940s, EX ....$450.00 C

Ice bucket, "Drink Coca-Cola In Bottles," 1960s, EX ....$20.00 D

Ice tongs from Coca-Cola Bottling Co., Green Castle, Indiana, has a 3-digit phone number, 1920s, EX......$500.00 D

"Jim Dandy" combination tool that has a screwdriver, button hook, cigar cutter, and bottle opener, rare, 1920, EX ....$300.00 D

Jug with paper label in original box, 1960s, one gallon, EX..............$40.00 D

Door lock, metal, "Drink Coca-Cola in Bottles, Delicious and Refreshing," 1930s, EX, $75.00 C. Courtesy of Mitchell collection.

Fact wheel, United States at a glance, EX, $95.00 C. Courtesy of Mitchell collection.

Jumbo straws in a box with the fishtail design, "Be Really Refreshed," 1960s, EX ....$75.00 C

Letter opener, metal and plastic with bottle on handle, 1950, red and white, EX ....$35.00 D

Letter opener, plastic, from Coca-Cola Bottling Co. Dyersburg, Tenn., clear, EX ....$20.00 C

Light fixture, rectangular, colored leaded glass, with bottom beaded fringe, "Coca-Cola 5¢," "Pittsburgh Mosaic Glass Co., Inc., Pittsburgh, Pa.," 1910, 11"w x 22" x 7½"h, G.........$6,000.00 C

Light, hanging adjustable, with popcorn insert on one of four sides, with red and white Coca-Cola advertising on the other panels, 1960s, 18" x 18", M .....$525.00 D

Light, octagonal hanging Art Deco motif, believed to have been made for the San Francisco World's Fair Exhibition in 1939, 1930s, 20"w x 24"t, EX..........$1,800.00 D

Magic lantern slide, hand colored glass, "A Home Run" from Advertising Slide Co., St. Louis, 1970s, EX ......$125.00 D

Magic lantern slide, hand colored glass, "Good Company!" features a couple toasting with Coke bottles, 1920s, EX ....$140.00 D

Globe, leaded glass, round, "Coca-Cola," rare, 1920s, EX, $10,000.00 D.

Magic lantern slide, hand colored glass, "People say they like it because ...," 1920s, EX................................$125.00 D

Magic lantern slide, hand colored glass "Stop at the Red Sign," Coca-Cola Bottling Co, Festus, Missouri, 1920s, EX..$135.00 D

Magic lantern slide, hand colored glass, "Unanimous good taste!," Festus, Missouri, 1920s, EX.....................$135.00 D

Message pad shaped like a case of Coke, 1980s, EX ....$20.00 D

Mileage meter, "Travel refreshed," originating from Asheville, North Carolina, white on red, 1950s, G...$500.00 C

Mileage meter with home location of Crescent Beach, South Carolina, also has bottom stamp Marion Coca-Cola Bottling Company, 1950s, VG ....$1,000.00 D

Money bag, vinyl zippered, "Enjoy Coca-Cola," 1960s, VG ....$12.00 C

Music box, cooler-shaped, in working order, 1950s, EX ....$145.00 C

Nail clippers, samples with advertising, EX...$20.00 D

Chewing gum display box, held twenty 5¢ packages, cardboard, rare, 1920s, VG, $1,500.00 B.

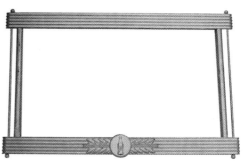

Wooden frame for 36" x 20" posters, 1940, EX, $275.00 D. Courtesy of Muddy River Trading Co./Gary Metz.

Notepad holder for candlestick phone, price includes phone which also has a courtesy coin box, 1920s, G...$300.00 C

Olympic disc in original box, 1980, M...$15.00 D

Paper cigar band with bottle logo, 1930s, EX..............................$55.00 C

Pen and pencil set by Cross with logo on pocket clips, in original case, M...$65.00 D

Pen and pencil set in plastic case celebrating the 50th anniversary of Coca-Cola Bottling in Frankfort, IN, 1965, EX...............................$75.00 D

Pencil holder, white with red button, 1950s, 5" tall, EX..................$300.00 D

Pencil, mechanical, 1930s, EX .$40.00 D

Pencil sharpener, cast metal in shape of bottle, 1930s, VG ....$40.00 C

Pencil sharpener, round, plastic, "Drink Coca-Cola," 1960s, white and red, EX ....$12.00 D

Pen, "Drink" and bottle on pocket clip, with prices for specific quantities on barrel, NM...............................$55.00 D

Pen, ink, red and white, 1950s, EX ....$45.00 D

Note pad holder for candlestick phone, price includes phone which also has a courtesy coin box, 1920s, EX, $900.00 B. Courtesy of Gary Metz.

Penlight, push button with wave logo, 1970s, white and red, EX.........$12.00 D

Pepsin gum jar with thumbnail type lid, 1910, EX.............................$1,600.00 B

Pin set, 100th Anniversary, limited edition, framed under glass, 1986, EX..$275.00 D

Pin set, 100th Anniversary, limited edition, framed under glass, 1986, G..$125.00 C

Plaque for dispenser steel, stepped corners, 1950s, 7" x 3", EX...........$75.00 D

Plastic slant front inkwell with black and red fountain pen, 1940 – 1950s, EX..$350.00 C

Play dollar bill, "Refresh Yourself At The Bar," NM.........................$90.00 D

Pocket protector, "Coke adds life to everything nice," 1960s, white and red, EX......................................$8.00 C

Pocket protector, vinyl, Union City, Tennessee, 1950s, red and black, G..$15.00 C

Mileage meter, "Travel refreshed," originating from Asheville, N.C., white on red, 1950s, EX, $1,550.00 B. Courtesy of Muddy River Trading Co./Gary Metz.

Hi-Fi premium record holder for 45rpm records, will hold 90 records, spinner on base for ease of turning to selections, 10" x 10¾", NM, $100.00 B. Courtesy of Autopia Advertising Auctions.

Polaroid camera, "Coke adds life to Happy Times," G......................$75.00 C

Polaroid camera, "Coke adds life to Happy Times," MIB...............$150.00 C

Popcorn bag, Jungleland, 5" x 14", NM.......................................$12.00 D

Postage stamp carrier, celluloid, 1902, EX ....$500.00 C

Postage stamp holder, celluloid, 1901 – 1902, 1½" x 2½", EX ....$575.00 C

Pot holder, "Drink Coca-Cola every bottle sterilized," red lettering on yellow, 1910 – 1912, G...............$275.00 C

Record album, "The Shadow," 1970, EX ....$35.00 C

Record carrier for 45 rpms, plastic and vinyl, 1960s, 9" x 8", red and white, VG ....$40.00 C

Record dust cover, Sgt. Preston, 1971, EX ....$35.00 D

Refrigerator bottle, "Compliments of Coca-Cola Bottling Company" on one side with two horses and riders on the other side, 1940 – 1950s, 9" tall, EX ....$125.00 C

Metal string holder with six pack in spotlight, "Take Home In Cartons," red, 1930s, 14" x 16", EX, $1,000.00 B.
Courtesy of Muddy River Trading Co./Gary Metz.

Polaroid camera, "Coke adds life to Happy Times," EX, $95.00 C.
Courtesy of Mitchell collection.

Refrigerator water bottle, green glass, "Compliments Coca-Cola Bottling Co.," embossed, G....................$75.00 C

Ricky Nelson set, consisting of poster and a 45LP, personally autographed, framed, difficult to find these, 1960s, 18" x 14½", G ....$275.00 C

Ruler, 12", plastic with wave logo, 1970, white and red, EX ....$5.00 D

Ruler, 12", wooden, "Coca-Cola refresca en grande," 1950 – 1960s, VG...$5.00 D

Salt and pepper shaker, thimble-shaped, 1920s, EX...............................$350.00 D

Sandwich toaster, "Coke," used at soda fountains to toast sandwiches and would imprint the bread, hard to find, 1930s, EX ....$1,950.00 D

Sewing needle case with packaging featuring the same model that appeared on the 1924 calendar, 1920s, EX......$75.00 C

Sewing needles in Coke packaging, featuring the girl at party with the fox fur, 1920s, EX...............................$75.00 C

School set, "Drink Coca-Cola Delicious Refreshing," complete with pencils, rulers, erasers in box, 1930s, red, EX ....$80.00 D

Refrigerator water bottle, green glass "Compliments Coca-Cola Bottling Co.," embossed, EX, $135.00 C. Courtesy of Mitchell collection.

Ricky Nelson set, consisting of poster and a 45LP, personally autographed, framed, difficult to find these, 1960s, 18" x 14½", EX, $575.00 B. Courtesy of Muddy River Trading Co./Gary Metz.

Shade, ceiling, milk glass with original hardware, 1930s, 10", EX ....$1,500.00 D

Shade, colored leaded glass, with the chain edge that originally had a border of hanging beaded fringe, "Property of the Coca-Cola Co. to be returned on demand," must be on top band, 1920s, 18" dia., VG ....$3,000.00 C

Shade, window, "Drink Coca-Cola, The Pause that Refreshes in Bottles," very rare, 4' x 7', VG ....$3,000.00 C

Shaving kit canvas bag with "Enjoy Coca-Cola" and the dynamic wave logo on the front, EX........................$25.00 C

Shoe spoon with wave logo, plastic, 1970s, white and red, EX ....$8.00 C

Shotgun, model 1500XLT, Coca-Cola Centennial, embossed Coca-Cola on receiver and barrel never fired, 1986, MIB ....$1,500.00 C

Statue holding bottles of Coca-Cola, "Tell me your profit story, please" on base, 1930 – 1940s, EX..........$150.00 C

Straws in box with titled bottle, EX..$65.00 C

Straws, with front side cut out for dispensing straws and the other three sides with bottle pictured, "Delicious and Refreshing," EX ....$175.00 C

Street marker, brass, "Drink Coca-Cola, Safety First," fairly rare piece, 1920, VG, $175.00 C. Courtesy of Mitchell collection.

Shade, colored leaded glass, with the chain edge that originally had a border of hanging beaded fringe, "Property of the Coca-Cola Co. to be returned on demand," must be on top band, 1920s, 18" dia., EX, $5,000.00 C.

Street marker, brass, "Drink Coca-Cola, Safety First," fairly rare piece, 1920, F ....$75.00 C

String dispenser, tin, red with carton in yellow circle, 12" x 16", EX ..$450.00 C

String holder, curved panels, "Take Home 25¢," six pack in spotlight, 1930s, NM...........................$1,000.00 C

Superman, original radio broadcast, EX ....$25.00 C

Syrup dispenser, reproduction, made of hard rubber, unusual piece, 1950s, EX ....$700.00 C

Tape for reel to reel for radio play, contains 16 advertising spots prepared by McCann & Erickson, Inc., New York, 1970s, VG ....$25.00 C

Tape measure, horseshoe-shaped, Coke advertising on side, NM.............$8.00 C

Tap knob, doubled sided, "Coke," 1960 – 1970, NM............................$25.00 D

Tap knob, enameled, double-sided, "Drink Coke or Coca-Cola, Ask for it Either Way," 1940 – 1950s, EX ....$85.00 C

Tap knob, one side, "Coca-Cola," 1970, EX ....$25.00 C

Telephone, bottle-shaped, new, MIB...$15.00 D

Light fixture, rectangular, colored leaded glass, with bottom beaded fringe, "Coca-Cola 5¢,"
"Pittsburgh Mosaic Glass Co., Inc., Pittsburgh, Pa.," 1910, 11"w x 22" x 7½"h, EX, $12,000.00 C.

Telephone, can-shaped, new, MIB...$25.00 D

Telephone in the shape of a 10 oz. bottle, EX.....................................$55.00 D

Thimble, aluminum, 1920s, F..$30.00 D

Thimble, "Coca-Cola," red lettering, M..$25.00 D

Tin napkin holder, foreign in origin, set up to resemble a box type cooler, 1940s, VG...$650.00 C

Training kit for sales complete with record, film strips, and charts, 1940s, EX...$125.00 D

Tumbler, showing "Drink Coca-Cola," 1950 – 1970s, EX....................$15.00 C

Tumbler, tulip shaped with syrup lines, EX...$40.00 D

Umbrella, "Drink Coca-Cola ... Be Really Refreshed," F..............$575.00 C

Umbrella, orange, black, and white, "Drink Coca-Cola," 1930s, EX...$800.00 C

Uncut sheet of coupons for Coca-Cola, EX...$25.00 C

Vinyl carrying bag with zipper top and the message "Drink Coca-Cola in bottles," 14" x 5" x 10", EX..........$20.00 C

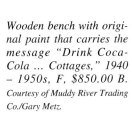

Tin napkin holder, foreign in origin, set up to resemble a box type cooler, 1940s, F, $525.00 B. *Courtesy of Muddy River Trading Co./Gary Metz.*

Wooden bench with original paint that carries the message "Drink Coca-Cola ... Cottages," 1940 – 1950s, F, $850.00 B. Courtesy of Muddy River Trading Co./Gary Metz.

Wall pocket, three-dimensional pressed fiber board, 9" x 13", EX .... $650.00 C

Water cup with handle, tin, "This cup for water but Drink Coca-Cola in Bottles, Coca-Cola Bottling Co. Greencastle, Ind." is printed in black in bottom of cup, rare piece, 1930s, EX .... $140.00 C

Winchester model #94, Coca-Cola Centennial, only 2,500 produced, never fired, 1986, MIB .... $1,500.00 C

Wooden bench with original paint that carries the message "Drink Coca-Cola ... Cottages," 1940 – 1950s, VG .... $1,000.00 C

Wooden frame for 36" x 20" posters, 1940, VG .... $225.00 C

Wooden Kay Displays frame with unusual crest at top, will accommodate 40" x 24" poster, 1930s, F .... $175.00 B

Wooden transistor radio with battery compartment behind back door, Philippines, 1940s, 7"w x 4"d x 5"t, EX .... $400.00 C

Wooden vertical original Coke frame with crest, gold, 1940s, EX .... $300.00 D

GARY METZ'S
MUDDY RIVER
TRADING CO.
METZ SUPERLATIVES AUCTION

Vintage and Antique Advertising
Tin • Paper • Cardboard • Porcelain
Country Store Items

MY SERVICES INCLUDE:

•Buying old advertising of every description•
•Finding and filling customer wants in advertising•
•Auction promotion and presentation•
•Single item or collection liquidation through consignment, on a fee or net basis•
•Restaurant decor services•
•Anything related to the buying, selling, or trading of antique advertising — we can talk•

ALWAYS WANTING TO BUY:

Collections • Signs in quantity • Coca-Cola • Die-Cuts • Stand Ups
Any single great sign or item priced from $500 to $25,000

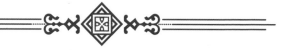

Gary Metz's
MUDDY RIVER TRADING CO.
METZ SUPERLATIVES AUCTION
P. O. Box 18185 • Roanoke, VA 24104
Phone: 540-725-4311